'The Servant Songs ... portion of the Word ... Dr. Stuart Sacks br... Scriptures, spiritual i... his exposition of these timeless passages. In thirteen short, readable chapters Sacks provides insight into the nature and work of Jesus as Israel's and our Messiah and offers encouragement for those who want to know him and be like him. It would be difficult for anyone to read this book and not be helped by it.'

*James Montgomery Boice*
*Tenth Presbyterian Church, Philadelphia*

Every generation needs good guides to key portions of the Scripture, and the Servant Songs of Isaiah, often referred to as the 'fifth gospel', are surely fundamental to our understanding of the person and work of the Messiah. Stuart Sacks, a Jewish believer from the USA, has provided Christians with a very accessible guide to the significance and application of these crucial passages. His Jewish insights are woven into the text of the book in an easy manner, and I heartily recommend it as a study aid for Christians who are serious about the Word of God.

*Walter Riggans*
*General Director*
*CMJ (Church's Ministry among Jewish People)*

'Writing as a Jewish Christian, Stuart Sacks provides a most valuable introduction to Isaiah's "Servant of the Lord". Built on a sound theological foundation, these non-technical meditations and reflections appeal to all who wish to understand better the identity and mission of Isaiah's Servant figure. The author's ability to move fluidly between the promises and prophecies of Isaiah and their New Testament fulfilment makes this an enlightening and practical book. Clearly, Stuart Sacks is thrilled to introduce us to his Messiah, and to encourage us all, Jew and Gentile alike, to know him and experience his infinite grace for ourselves.'

*John S Ross*
*Christian Witness to Israel*

'Stuart Sacks brings the prophet Isaiah and his message to our day. It is a message the church needs to hear.'

*R C Sproul*
*Ligonier Ministries*

# REVEALING JESUS AS MESSIAH

A Portrait of the Messiah
and His People

## Stuart D Sacks

Christian Focus

© Stuart D. Sacks
ISBN 1-85792-311-1

Published in 1998 by Christian Focus Publications Ltd
Geanies House, Fearn, Ross-shire
IV20 1TW, Scotland, Great Britain

Cover design by Donna Macleod

# CONTENTS

| BC | Israel (Northern kingdom) Kings | Prophets | Judah (Southern kingdom) Prophets | Kings |
|---|---|---|---|---|
| 841 | Jehu | | Joel | Athaliah |
| | Jehoahaz | | | Joash |
| | Jehoash | Jonah | | Amaziah |
| | Jereboam II | Amos | | Azariah |
| | | Hosea | | (Uzziah) |
| 753 | Zechariah | | | |
| | Shallum | | | Jotham |
| | Menahem | | Isaiah | |
| | Pekahiah | | | Ahaz |
| | Pekah | | | |
| | Hoshea | | | |
| 722 | Kingdom overthrown | | Micah | |
| | by Assyria | | | Hezekiah |
| | | | | Manasseh |
| | | | Nahum | |
| | | | | Amon |
| | | | Zephaniah | Josiah |
| 642 | | | Jeremiah | |
| | | | Habakkuk | |
| | | | | Jehoahaz |
| | | | | Jehoiakim |
| | | | Daniel | Jehoiachin |
| | | | Ezekiel | Zedekiah |
| 586 | | | Kingdom overthrown by Babylonia | |

# Preface

It's been nearly forty years since I studied and worshipped in what was one of my home town's oldest structures, *Beth Emeth* Synagogue.[1] Located in the heart of the inner city, I drove by it recently to observe the massive red-stoned building, now abandoned and boarded up. I thought back to the many Sabbaths spent there, remembering bits and pieces of liturgy and textbooks. I could still recall the old rabbi's voice with its carefully measured cadences and occasional drone-like character. Somehow his thoughts always seemed a bit too erudite for someone of my tender years. My fondest memory of him was the evening he prayed with me. I had been a troublesome teenager and had managed to run afoul of the law. I sought out the rabbi and we prayed that God would get me on the right path and help me turn away from anything evil.

Finding the power to lead a godly life was somewhat more problematic.

Although there were no more conflicts with the police, there was an inner conflict yet to be resolved: my conscience was devoid of peace. Many years would pass before I turned to the pages of Scripture and learned of Him who was pierced for my transgressions and crushed for my iniquities, whose punishment procured my peace.

A chief obstacle to my belief in Jesus (the New Testament's equivalent to Joshua) was what seemed to be its 'unJewishness'. In the twelfth century AD, the Jewish scholar Maimonedes wrote thirteen principles to help characterize the essence of Judaism. The third of these statements declares that God is incorporeal. For the Jewish mind, the idea of God assuming human form has an idolatrous ring to it. And for many Jews, the very notion is something that only an unenlightened Gentile mind could entertain. From Judaism's perspective, then, the New Testament's proclamation might be branded the 'Gospel according to St. Plato', but it could hardly be considered anything of Semitic origin.

Notwithstanding, the writers of the New Testament were Jewish. Its most prolific writer was a rabbi 'extremely zealous for the traditions' of his fathers (Gal. 1:14).

For years I dismissed the Christian faith as little more than an irrelevant aberration.

But God had not dismissed me. Through spiritually lean and hungry years He led me back to the Person I had once cast aside. His perseverance drew me to Him who was once despised but is now enthroned as 'a priest forever' (Ps. 110:4). His love re-connected me with my Jewish roots.

The Almighty refers to a number of ancient

personages as His servants, such as Abraham, Moses, Caleb and Joshua. They devotedly served God with distinction. But among those servants whose wills were swallowed up in their Master's, none was called upon to suffer so grievously – and innocently – as Job. Job stands closest to Isaiah's prophetical 'Servant' as an innocent, even righteous, sufferer. As such he experiences the cruel rejection of men in the midst of his awful ordeal (Job 16:10f.). Yet he suffered, as the French expositor, Dhorme, observed, from a cause that was wrapped up in mystery. Isaiah's Messianic Servant offered His life as *asham*, an expiatory offering (53:10) – the righteous on behalf of the godless. The experience of Job dissociates completely the question of sin and that of suffering; Job did not suffer for his own sin or for the sin of others. But the sorrows of Isaiah's Servant stem directly from the pervasive evil that characterises each of our lives. He suffered on behalf of our iniquities to satisfy the demands of divine justice.

It is to the Messiah that this humble volume is dedicated. I still marvel that God loves me to the extent that He would personally bear all the consequences of my foul thoughts and deeds. My praise for Him extends beyond the realm of forgiveness. Through His word and deed I've received a perspective on life which makes sense out of an otherwise chaotic and senseless

9

existence. To borrow a thought from C. S. Lewis, I believe in the gospel as I believe the sun has risen, not only because I see it, but because by it I see everything else.

*A word of apology to the reader regarding occasional quotations or references which, owing to my failure to carefully record or remember all of my resources, have not been footnoted.*

# 1

# The times and heart of Isaiah

With at least 800 occurrences in the Old
Testament, the term, *servant*, carries with it a wide
range of meaning and application. Primarily,
*ebhed* denotes one whose will is swallowed up in
another's – in other words, a slave. Yet it is
important to note that in ancient Israel the term
did not necessarily bear all the negative
connotations associated with it today. Moreover,
the title has a grand element as well, and it is this
aspect of servanthood which Isaiah develops
extensively as he reflects upon not only the
privilege of serving God but also the immense
cost bound up with that service. Studying his
words about the one called *Ebhed Yahweh* (The
Servant of the Lord) is more than an excursion
into servanthood, it is an in-depth presentation of
the ideal Servant whose appearance Isaiah longs
to see.

Isaiah received his revelation about 'The
Servant of the Lord' during a bleak period in
Israel's history. He was one of many bold
spokesmen raised up by God in the eighth and
seventh centuries BC whose messages were

couched against the fall of Israel to the Assyrians and, later, Judah to the Babylonians. The words of Amos, Hosea, Micah, and Isaiah addressed the impending Assyrian crisis while the fall of Judah served as the backdrop for the writings of Zephaniah, Nahum, Habakkuk, and Jeremiah.

Isaiah ministered the word of God in Jerusalem for more than forty years. He was married (his wife is called a prophetess, 8:3), had at least two children (named in 7:3 and 8:3), and was of noble birth. If tradition is correct, he died a martyr's death by being sawed in two.

The northern tribes (called 'Israel' since the breakup of Solomon's kingdom) were carried off captive by the Assyrians in 722 BC, an event Isaiah knew was coming (6:11-13). But God revealed the certainty of another crisis as well. Through his prophetic oracles Isaiah tells of Babylon's conquest of the southern tribes of Judah and their deportation as well, an awful reality occurring more than a century after Isaiah's death. It was against the context of that exile that Isaiah pens his most eloquent and penetrating words of hope, beginning with chapter 40, launching what is often called the *Book of Comfort*. He tells his people and future generations that God's love for them has not been extinguished by their sin. With supernatural precision, he prophesies the rise to power of a Persian liberator, Cyrus, God's anointed agent who will, long after Isaiah's death, restore the people to their native land. Over and above that, however, a greater messianic deliverer fills the prophet's vision of future blessings; that revelation appears in distinctive portions of Isaiah focusing on God's Messiah-Servant. These passages (sometimes called the *Servant Songs*) are found in chapters 42, 49, 50, and 53 (beginning at 52:13).

Augustine called Isaiah 'the fifth Gospel', yet, in truth, it is the first Gospel. Here is the earliest comprehensive presentation of the Messiah's miraculous birth, sinless life, atoning death, and glorious exaltation – all on behalf of a perverted, lost world. Studying the *Servant Songs* will bring us face-to-face with Him who is the focal point of saving faith. Other texts from Isaiah will also be helpful to that end, especially parts of chapters 40 and 61. The former chapter sets the stage for the coming of God's Servant; the latter, while not employing the title, *servant*, is nonetheless of pivotal importance, Jesus having quoted it at the outset of His ministry at Nazareth's synagogue (Luke 4:16-21).

In Isaiah's day, heroism found its primary expression in sophomoric wine drinking and debauchery; many were 'mighty' in mixing drinks (5:22). Injustice and perversion were charges levelled against a nation that had been called by God to love and serve Him (Deut. 6:4-9). But we are ill-advised to point a condemning finger against Israel. Honesty commands us to see ourselves in them; we have all sinned and have forsaken the Lord in innumerable ways. In his book, *The Training of the Twelve*, A. B. Bruce speaks of the kind of popular religion whose creed permits people to think fine thoughts without requiring anything noble from them; 'it substitutes romancing about heroism in the place of being heroes.' There is an old Russian proverb that no man is a hero to his valet. And none of us can stand heroically when measured by the exacting requirements of God's holiness.

It is the heart-felt recognition of that truth that drives us to desire the Servant of the Lord's ministry on our behalf. As we read Isaiah let us remember that it is the Messiah-Servant's work alone that saves us.

Archbishop William Temple squarely hit the mark when he said, 'The only thing of my very own which I contribute to my redemption is the sin from which I need to be redeemed.' But let us also recall that the Prince of Servants has sent us into the world as servants and has commanded us to be like Him (John 17:18). The road to greatness is the way of servanthood (Mark 10:43-44), the nature of which is defined by the life of Jesus Christ. Although His perfect servanthood alone can bring redemption, we must not lose sight of the fact that the principles governing His life are binding upon all who love Him. Wherever applicable, we should try to see the relevance of Isaiah's vision of servanthood to all who desire, albeit imperfectly, to model their life after the Savior's. This is only right, for Jesus wants the world to see the grace and power of His life revealed in ours.

# 2

# Preparing for the Servant

587 BC was a disastrous time for the people of Jerusalem and Judah. More than a century earlier the northern tribes of Israel were conquered and carried away by the Assyrians. Now the Babylonians laid waste the southern territories and a seventy-year exile uprooted the nation. Shameful idolatry had caused the undoing of the people. Innumerable warnings incited only an unresponsive disdainfulness; the prophets were considered fools (Hos. 9:7). God, who never threatens in vain, allowed the axe to fall (Isa. 1:7).

It was the 'cup of wrath' of which the prophet Jeremiah had tirelessly warned Judah for twenty-three years (Jer. 25:3). Now all had become a desolate wasteland; long silenced were the sounds of joy and gladness (Jer. 25:10-11); Isaiah's prophecy to Hezekiah (39:5-7) had become an irrefutable fact.

*Nahamu, nahamu ammi,* begins Isaiah's cry (40:1), as he sees beyond the shame and degradation of a fallen nation to the God whose grace is sufficient to reclaim even the most obdurate of them. Here is the word of God coming to break the yet future bondage of Israel whose sin and wretchedness find their counterparts in all the peoples of the world.

## Who were they?

They were a people reminded of their frailty, whose substance was no more resilient than the withering grass – whose 'glory' was as faded as fallen flowers (40:6-7). Physical and moral frailty are interconnected. When Isaiah says, 'Surely, grass is the people,' he affirms the link between our weakness and the judgment of a holy God. His word stands against us and we are mowed down by its righteous indignation (cf. Ps. 90:7). Like Israel we have spurned and forsaken God (1:4). We have turned our backs on Him, rejecting His counsel, ignoring His Law.

Ironically, these charges are levelled against a people whose religious lives are extraordinarily active, whose calendars are filled with festivals, feasts and assemblies. Few things are more difficult to detect than corruption clothed in religiosity. But God knows the heart and says their activities are a burden to Him; He tells them to stop bringing their meaningless offerings (1:13-14). They fasted, yet while ostensibly seeking God, permitted and even practiced social evils (58:3-5).

A well-known preacher observed that he never

knew a person who consciously wanted to be evil. The great mystery of godlessness is to be seen in the fact that individuals fail so miserably while they're trying to be good. Isaiah marvels that his people, so badly bruised, would persist in rebelling against the Lord (1:5). But that is the pathetic realism of sinfulness: we're beaten half-dead yet ripe for more chastisement.

> 'For all this His anger is not turned away,
> But His hand is stretched out still' (10:4, NKJV).[2]

When we've come to the point in our lives where we know something of the deep pollutedness within us – and the impossibility of rooting it out even by the most intense human effort – we're ready to take seriously our Lord's words, 'Apart from Me you can do nothing' (John 15:5). When we honestly consider what we are in contrast to what God wants us to be, the odds of making such a lofty transition seem formidably stacked against us. There are those, like the affluent young ruler, who applaud their moral accomplishments ('all these things have I done', Luke 18:21); others bring salve to their consciences by comparing themselves to those on the lower ebb of society (Luke 18:11). But for those whom Jesus loves, His word cuts through their sham of self-righteousness and reveals its essence: despicably filthy rags (Isa. 64:6). Everything we do, including the acts which benefit

18

others, flows from our fallen nature. The Spirit of God alone enables us to know the deceitfulness of our hearts and the folly of trying to justify ourselves before a God of absolute moral purity (Isa. 6:3).

**What has happened to us?**
Sin has mortally wounded our hearts. When the Messiah preached His first sermon He said He had been sent 'to release the oppressed' (Luke 4:18, cf. Isa. 61:1). Poignant words of comfort are directed to those who thought their cause and needs were of no concern to God (40:27). Tender words of consolation are heard: their sin has been paid for; it is a message impressed 'upon the heart of Jerusalem' (40:2). Ample proof of its divine trustworthiness will be seen in the nation's return to their homeland. But much more is involved than that.

Are we to surmise that the punishment of Israel thoroughly satisfied the demands of divine justice? Is it enough to believe that reconciliation could be effected by the stern discipline of a generation of Israelites? 'Their sin has been paid for' (40:2) is couched in what scholars call 'the prophetic past', suggesting a provision made long before the exile. What was paid and by whom is the grand theme of Isaiah's 'Servant' passages. The essence of the overall message is not that people have been set at liberty to return to their homeland (as meaningful as that is) but, rather, that God has

19

come to them, assuring them that they have been pardoned on the basis of what He has done on their behalf.

Isaiah prepared the hearts of the people for this great news when he spoke earlier of *Immanuel* (chapter 7), of the supernatural Child (chapter 9), and of the fruitful *Branch*, anointed with the Spirit of the Lord (chapter 11).

Because of the collective references to Israel as God's servant (41:8; 49:3), some have tried to see the nation as God's servant in all of Isaiah's 'Songs'. But the idea of a corporate servant breaks down at two crucial points: first, when Israel's service is said to have failed – she is 'deaf and blind' (42:19) – and second, when the final 'Song' (52:13-53:12) so clearly identifies Him as an individual who suffers in the place of His rebellious people. This is not to deny Israel's role as God's servant. However, the nation's servanthood must be sustained by the grace of God; and that animating support flows to the nation through their Messiah, in whom the glory of the Lord is revealed (40:5). Even when the restored faithful remnant returned from captivity they were unable to attain the idealistic goals of purity and righteousness required of a true servant of God (see Isaiah 58–59). The stern judgment of captivity had not produced in the remnant of the restoration period a thoroughly refined and obedient people. But in the eyes of those who witnessed the words and works of Jesus, all the criteria of holiness finally found their genuine expression:

> 'Jesus had become a remnant of one... As the embodiment of the faithful remnant, He would undergo divine judgment for sin (on the cross), endure an exile (three days forsaken by God in the grave), and experience a restoration (resurrection) to life as the foundation of a new Israel, inheriting the promises of God afresh. As the remnant restored to life, He becomes the focus of the hopes for the continued existence of the people of God in a new kingdom, a new Israel of Jew and Gentile alike.'[3]

Israel traditionally looked to her leaders in times of national crises. But all of them were carried off; none remained. What will a people do when every visible authority is no more? What options do you have when all of society's structures have collapsed? Centuries before, David had asked much the same question as he witnessed his own society in decay (Ps. 11:3). Again, the weakness of the nation is painfully evident: Jerusalem's walls were breached, the city emptied of life, its few remaining citizens the objects of enemy jests and taunts. In the midst of sadness and dismay a messenger from Heaven's court is heard: 'Comfort My people.' Over against the people's frailty a triumphant word is given: 'The Sovereign Lord comes with power' (40:10). Israel's impotence (witnessing, as it does, to the powerlessness of man) must point us away from man to Him who alone has the power to save. Isaiah's vision celebrates the only real strength in the universe. 'Stop trusting in man,' is more than good advice (2:22); it is the repudiation of everything unworthy of our faith. When God takes away from us all 'supply and support' (3:1) He does so that even the best of us will finally confess, 'I have no remedy' (3:7). We must be emptied of all confidence in ourselves and in others. To bring us to that point often requires much painful divestiture. Until the events of our lives have brought us up against the wall and all our resources dried up and flown away, we have not fully understood the greatness of His incredible love. It is when the chariots are in front of us and the Red Sea behind us that we have the unique opportunity to trust God in more than an abstract, impersonal manner. In such a place and time only the faithful word of God remains (40:8); upon it alone we are compelled to rely. Like all the prophets, Isaiah affirms the timeless truth that God requires His people to live by faith in His word, even when the physical evidences of His tender care are far from obvious or even contradicted by our senses.

## Setting the stage
Desperation of this magnitude helped set the stage for the appearance of God's Servant, the extension

of God's 'arm' to His people (40:10). Although King Cyrus is given the name 'shepherd' (44:28), his role in restoring the captives to Judah functions within limited parameters. He is a mini-messiah, not the Shepherd whose strong yet gentle arms carry the lambs close to his heart (40:11); Cyrus has no paternal regard for the weak or the helpless.

We may well imagine God's Servant, 'that great Shepherd of the sheep' (Heb. 13:20), leading His flock along the wilderness 'highway' (40:3), directing and protecting His own. As Isaiah views the circuitous route, it is certain that the prophet is not primarily concerned with changes in the landscape (40:3ff.); he yearns to see God's grace build up the devastated wastelands of people's lives. For sin has turned the world into a wilderness. And it is precisely there – in our personal desert – that God comes to us with His word of grace. His word is full of comfort for it assures us that He will not abandon us to that restless, inhospitable place. It is for this reason that men like David were constrained to seek Him in the midst of oppressive dryness. Because His love is better than life, desiring God's presence was the psalmist's priority – even in the Judean desert (Ps. 63).

God intends His powerful word to exercise benevolent control over us, even altering our dispositions. But that is not the chief reason for our comfort. God tells us that our 'hard service is ended'; our 'sin has been paid for' (40:2). Isaiah's 'gospel' is simply this: our past has been dealt with; we need not allow our bruised consciences to torture us with remembrances of failures and disobedience. The good resolutions gone bad, the thoughtless, rebellious acts – all are consigned to the forgotten past. God chose us to be His servants (41:9). Though we've been unprofitable and unfaithful, even stubborn and blind, He loved us and chose us before the creation of the world (Eph. 1:4). Having loved us so well and so long, it is inconceivable that He should let us go – 'to the praise of His glorious grace' (Eph. 1:6).

No-one who spells God with a capital 'G' ever imagines Him growing 'tired or weary' (Isa. 40:28). But perhaps we fear that He may one day grow tired of us. I have often grown tired of me. I'm tired of my sin and of the fact that, after three decades as a believer, so many rough places remain in my life. Were it not for the work of the Servant I would have no reason to hope that God's patient love will never forsake me. How singularly fortunate that Isaiah says (reading with the KJV), 'His reward is with Him and His work before Him' (40:10). The reward is the Messiah's and the work is His. I need only trust in what He has done for me. I must never forget that He loved me before I was born and accepts me solely on the basis of what His strong arm has accomplished on my behalf.

**The greatest news ever**
News of this calibre is not intended to be the sole property of a select few.

Chapter forty's opening verbs are plural (we are collectively to tell of God's comfort); and the ninth verse envisions Zion as a whole heralding the gospel: 'You who bring good tidings ... lift up your voice with a shout.' There's no greater news in all of creation than this: God, Himself, has wiped out our sins. It's worth shouting about – to the end that many may hear and believe!

# 3

## Behold My Servant, whom I uphold
### *Isaiah 42:1-4*

Multiple images may be associated with Isaiah's *Servant* passages.

As previously observed, Israel cannot be excluded from the meaning of the term. Rabbinic scholars, noting the word's individualistic aspect, have sought the Servant's identity in such figures as Jeremiah, Cyrus, Zerubbabel, and even Isaiah, himself. While it is true that Isaiah does not explicitly link the title 'Messiah' with the 'Servant of the Lord,' none who take the overall witness of the Scriptures seriously can doubt that both figures refer to the same person. Even within the writings of Isaiah it is clear that both figures are uniquely anointed (61:1); each brings light unto the Gentiles (55:4; cf. 49:6); neither is pretentious in His first appearance (7:14, 15; 11:1; cf. 53:2; 42:3); and the title of Davidic 'branch' rests upon them both (11:1-4). Equally significant are the dual facts of their humiliation and exaltation (49:7; 52:13-15). Undeniably, Jesus saw the blueprint for His ministry in Isaiah's *Servant* (Luke 22:37).

## The Source of the Servant's Power

God says He delights in His Servant (42:1). A voice from heaven confirmed this when Jesus was baptized by John in the Jordan (Mark 1:11). Jesus' baptism was not, as it has been for so many, a symbolic testimony of repentance and faith; rather, it was an occasion marking Heaven's full acceptance of His life. For thirty years He had lived an inconspicuous life. But He had lived those many years in perfect fellowship with His Father. By the age of twelve Jesus knew that the service of His Father took first place. And that dedication controlled every aspect of His life, culminating in a three-year ministry in which He completed the work assigned Him as God's 'righteous Servant' (53:11). Well did Isaiah say of the Servant, 'He shall draw His breath in the fear of the Lord' (11:3).

We know Jesus was born into a world where He enjoyed no human advantage. He could not turn to family position or rank or influential friends, the resources we so naturally look to for help in achieving our purposes. Neither did He clutch at the prerogatives of Deity; Jesus 'made Himself nothing' (Phil. 2:6-7). From the outset God's Messiah drew strength from the Spirit's inexhaustible storehouse. In essence, He abandoned Himself to the will of His Father. It was enough that the Spirit of the Lord rested upon Him, the Spirit of wisdom and might (Isa. 11:2).

God, who is faithful, held His Servant fast (42:1). Each of us has an innate tendency to want to control every aspect of his life. Now in my late-fifties, I can imagine a time when I will not be able to provide for my own needs but may have to depend fully on the mercy of others. These thoughts distress me, even though my Savior tells me not to be anxious about tomorrow (Matt. 6:34). I am helped in my struggle not only by His words but also by His life: Isaiah's Servant abandoned Himself totally to the will of God. His life of quiet submission stands as the Eternal's testimony to what it means to live by faith.

Like my Master, I must consciously be refreshed in the fact of the Father's love for me and His invitation to me to cast all of my anxieties upon Him (1 Pet. 5:7).

Isaiah also speaks of Abraham's descendants as God's servant (41:8-9). It is evident that the prophet is thinking of individuals who, like the nation's first patriarch, have been called to know and serve God. God promises to uphold all those whom He has chosen, even taking them by the hand in the midst of strife (41:10-11). He is committed to sustain us in our desolate places (41:18). The ancient rabbis, referring to Isaiah 12:3, spoke of drawing forth from God's Spirit ('from the wells of salvation') as an occasion for great joy. No foundation is more firmly established than this: God desires to work supernaturally in and through His people. It is a very personal work, as seen in the gentle caress of the Shepherd (40:11) – His strong supportive hand (41:10). We will have occasion to reflect more on the 'covenantal' aspect of this truth when we consider the complementary writings of the prominent prophets of the Exile, Jeremiah and Ezekiel.

When the Jewish people returned to Palestine under the edict of the Persian king, Cyrus (538 BC), they faced the formidable task of rebuilding their decimated city and Temple. One prominent in the immense project, Zerubbabel, was given God's principle for success in the work through the prophet, Zechariah: 'Not by might nor by power [i.e., human resources], but by My Spirit...' (4:6). Since we do not draw from the Holy Spirit as perfectly as our Savior, flawless decision-making is not something we do regularly. But one thing is certain: our sovereign God wants us to seek His Spirit's help in all situations, even when our challenge appears (as in the case of Zerub-babel) to be largely physical in nature. It is not hard for theologians to construct a doctrine concerning the Holy Spirit, yet it is difficult to remember that, as believers, we are to find our strength through the Spirit's power within us (Eph. 3:16), and ask our heavenly Father for His anointing (Luke 11:13). Lamentably, far too many of us fail to make this our daily priority.

## The Nature of the Servant's Work

'He shall bring forth justice to the nations' (42:1). *Mishpat*, rendered 'justice,' encompasses the idea of judgment but, more fundamentally, the law (the *Torah*) which was to go forth from Jerusalem (2:3). The Messiah will bring the rule of God to all nations. Recently, a prominent rabbi was interviewed on a major network TV show. He commented on the need to establish justice, quoting God's command from Deuteronomy 16:20: *Tzedek, tzedek tirdoph* ('Justice, justice pursue!'). Then the rabbi noted that the Torah's text did not speak of the perfect accomplishment of justice, only its pursuit. Although he was unaware of it, his accurate exposition only served to underscore mankind's need for the Messiah. Steven Emerson (who often writes commentaries for the secular press concerning the Middle East) found significance in the fact that following the assassination of Yitzhak Rabin, nearly all Israelis were 'engaged in critical introspection about the existence of an evil presence within their society.' In his article (appearing in *The Wall Street Journal* around that time) Emerson states that 'the ultimate test of a society's soul is the extent to which it engages in critical self-analysis to root out evil.' Yet the task is like trying to root out a cancer after it has thoroughly metastasized. The Bible places little confidence in man's ability to achieve justice (Isa. 59:8-9). For true justice depends upon the establishment of righteousness (from the same Hebrew word as justice), which only the 'zeal of the Lord of hosts' can make a reality (9:6-7). We eagerly await God's 'new heavens and a new earth' when we will no longer 'toil in vain' (65:17, 23).

Until the time of his call to serve the Lord, Matthew was a civil servant; he had first-hand knowledge of corruption and the perversion of justice. Even when enforced impartially, Rome's law had little regard for the needs of individuals. When Matthew reflected upon the opening verses of Isaiah 42, he saw more than the establishment of courtroom justice. Along with the other disciples he had heard Jesus say that 'repentance and forgiveness of sins will be preached in His name to all nations, beginning at Jerusalem' (Luke 24:47). The message springing forth from the Holy City would embrace something so grand that even the remote Gentiles would anticipate its proclamation (Isa. 42:4). Matthew says the recipients of that message would put their hope 'in His Name' (Matt. 12:21). The farthest islands are drawn to a Person who reveals the law in its fulness; He embodies the essence of the law. It is no small matter to realize that Matthew saw the relevance of Isaiah 42 in the context of Jesus' healing the sick who followed Him (Matt. 12:15). What stood before Matthew was more than legal principles; he saw the personal expression of

God's mercy, a God whose forgiveness could be realized most tangibly.

Since this is the kind of God we serve, it is imperative that we imitate His tenderness and never lose track of the fact that He has revealed Himself to us as the source of all genuine hope. If only we treated others the way God treats us, we would be 'like a spring of water, whose waters do not fail' (58:11). Fresh water and salt water cannot flow from the same spring; God's servants must never allow both blessings and cursings to flow through them (James 3:10-11). History overflows with the stagnant waters of our cruelty. Heaven weeps over the resulting stench.

## The Character of the Servant

'He will not shout or cry out or raise His voice in the streets' (42:2). The expression, 'cry out,' brings to mind the fearlessly raised voices telling of man's weakness and God's saving strength (40:6ff). God's servants should seek to boldly tell of the wonders of God's grace. But God's Servant-Messiah does not come as an orator-debater; neither do we see Him advertising and promoting Himself. When Jesus ushered in the kingdom of God, He did not use manipulative or coercive means. His disciples even hear Him instruct others to be silent concerning Him (Matt. 12:16); He knows that His Father will see to the revelation of His identity at just the right time.

No one understood or more thoroughly practiced the doctrine of God's sovereignty than Jesus. He was never anxious about the outcome of His mission. Quietness and calmness come to those who have learned to entrust themselves and their work unto a sovereign God. The Almighty counsels us not to 'make haste' (as the KJV has it); in modern terms we might read Isaiah's words, 'The one who trusts will not panic' (28:16).

## Codes or compassion?

The ancient law code of Hammurabi is recognized as civilization's oldest codification of laws, antedating the Mosaic by several centuries. Although it is concerned with the administration of justice for Babylonian society, it is clear that consideration for property takes precedence over concern for humans. King Hammurabi's priorities find their modern expression in the thinking of today's multitudes who put an inordinately high value on things (so-called tangible possessions) while discounting the infinite value of individuals – of souls.

Although Jesus taught large crowds, His deepest work centered on the conversion and care of individuals. He did not think it a waste of time to invest Himself in a rather small group of followers. We need to carefully develop and cherish our personal relationships, investing time in them as one would if he were engaged in the making of a great work of art. Our Lord spent three years teaching the twelve (even though one of them totally rejected what he had been taught). Above all, He demonstrated a patient, gentle concern for them. A. B. Bruce, in his *Training of the Twelve*, spoke of the disciples as formerly 'ignorant' and 'narrow-minded,' full of 'prejudices, misconceptions, and animosities.' Some were not unlike bruised reeds (Isa. 42:3) in desperate need of restoration.

Still others who attended to the Master's words were like dying embers, whose last spark of hope was virtually extinguished. To these Jesus made real the word of the psalmist, 'The Lord is close to the brokenhearted and saves those who are crushed in spirit' (Ps. 34:18). He comes not to break off or snuff out but to heal and revitalize. He is like the Samaritan who pours oil on the helpless wounded (Luke 10:34). This is also the ministry that the Savior committed to His disciples (Luke 10:9). Jesus' concern for the whole person parallels Isaiah's burden in that our Lord desires us to 'satisfy the afflicted soul' (Isa. 58:10). We are His representatives, bringing God's word of relief to those who need to be reconciled to Him (2 Cor. 5:20).

**The Confidence of the Servant**
The Messiah knew that the Father had granted Him authority over all people that He might give

eternal life to all those whom the Father had given Him (John 6:37-39). Thus could Isaiah state, 'He will not falter or be discouraged' (42:4).

Large results, and those achieved quickly, seem to be the primary criteria whereby the 'success' of an individual (or work) is evaluated. That approach tends to be sadly superficial. William Carey, whose ministry in India touched and transformed so many lives, invested seven hard years of his life before seeing one Indian believe the gospel. While the United States Post Office was polling America, trying to decide whether to memorialize a fat or thin Elvis Presley on a first-class stamp, India's government was honoring Carey with its own postage stamp for his inestimable contribution to the nation's literary development. Carey's perseverance was the product of his trust in God's promises assuring him that ultimately his Savior's cause would triumph.

Jesus coined an expression to gently chide His own, calling them 'little-faiths' (Luke 12:28). Although their faith would become more rock-like, it was the Servant-Messiah who possessed unlimited spiritual power (John 3:34). Only that authority could establish the justice of God in a way that brought resilient hope to a guilty, sinful world. Israel is encouraged to meet her adversaries with the knowledge that although she is no more than a 'worm,' God Himself will help her (Isa. 41:14). All confidence stems from grace. It must, for the Law calls us to a level of obedience beyond our capabilities (Matt. 5:48). Its glory, like that reflected from the face of Moses, causes us to recoil in fear. Only the Servant-Messiah has flawlessly met its standards. His glory, while reflecting the truth, is also full of grace (John 1:14).

The reason for our confidence before God is that Jesus welcomes sinners into His fellowship (Luke 15:1-2). At best we are poor in spirit, hungering and thirsting after righteousness. God gives us what we so desperately need, promising to fill us (Matt. 5:6) as He more than compensates for the crushing weight of our own personal failures.

Israel looked to God when all the chips were down and there was no place else to go. It was in the midst of a vain existence that I first cried out to God for relief. How remarkable that even then He condescends to welcome us. He runs to embrace the lost son despite the fact that his repentance actually began in his belly (Luke 15:16-17).

# 4

# A Covenant to the People ...
# A Light to the Gentiles
*Isaiah 42:5-7*

In the opening verses of the chapter we learn of God's delight in His Servant (v. 1) and of the anointing of the Spirit that would constantly undergird His ministry (v. 2). Messiah's gentleness, patience, and quiet confidence would form the backdrop against which God's revelation (His *Torah*) would be established on the earth (vv. 3-4).

We now hear God speak to His Servant in a way that bolsters our confidence in the completion of His immense task. Isaiah reminds us of the fathomless greatness of Him 'who created the heavens and stretched them out, who spread out the earth and all that comes out of it, who gives breath to its people, and life to those who walk on it' (v. 5). The Talmud says that the world was created for the Messiah,[4] yet the New Testament moves us far beyond that thought, asserting that the Messiah is the one by whom 'all things were created: things in heaven and on earth, visible and invisible, whether thrones or powers or rulers or authorities; all things were created by Him and for Him' (Col. 1:16).

We live at a time when men, in denial of their creatureliness, have little if any appreciation of the fact that the earth and everything in it belongs to the Lord (Ps. 24:1). The blight of humanism has resulted in man thanking himself – his own cleverness and ingenuity – rather than 'God the LORD' (Isa. 42:5) for life's blessings. Even 'religious' thinkers err in their understanding of God's presence in His creation. Physicist Paul Davies, former winner of the prestigious Templeton Prize (for his contribution to religious thought), has written impressively showing that the universe exhibits a clear design and purpose. His well-developed contention is that it is inconceivable that the observable created order could have come about spontaneously; a creative power must have been molding and overseeing the process. Unfortunately, Davies reaches a disconcerting conclusion as well: God cannot be both omnipotent and personal. At this point the professor serves as an example of Albert Einstein's observation that most scientists make very poor philosophers. It is ironic that, in attempting to ascribe greatness to God, Davies makes Him far too small. The deity of his theories cannot begin to satisfy the deepest needs and aspirations of man. For unless God is involved personally in our lives we can only make wild guesses concerning His plan for creation – and us! Perhaps Dr. Davies does not want a personal

God getting too close to him (that may infringe upon his 'freedom'). David speaks joyfully for all generations of believers in his affirmation: 'You have laid Your hand upon me' (Ps. 139:5).

For the Servant, also, life's choicest blessing was bound up with God's promise, 'I will take hold of Your hand' (42:6); and it is a promise that the Messiah extends to all who trust in Him (John 10:29). The One who bears the weight of the government of the world upon His shoulders (Isa. 9:6) is surely able to bear the burdens of your life as well. The more we reflect upon His Person as revealed to us in Scripture the more we realize how willing He is to shoulder all of our concerns, even those which may seem to be little more than molehills on our life's bumpy landscape.

As the Author of life, it is God's right to govern as He sees fit. Having chosen the best means to meet His creatures' needs, we are assured that God's infinite resources will make His provisions effective for His people.

Isaiah knows that God often accomplishes His purposes through people who are ignorant of their role in implementing God's plans. Cyrus' meteoric rise to power and his remarkable victories were the Almighty's accomplishments although the Persian king did not acknowledge his unseen benefactor (Isa. 45:4-5). His people are witnesses to the irresistible might of the Lord; even in their rebelliousness they are living testimonies to the uniqueness of His saving power – to the God whose actions are irreversible (43:11-13).

Having called His Servant for a righteous purpose (42:6a), there can be no doubt that the Father will achieve all that He has determined to do through His Anointed One.

**The Covenant of Light**

Personal support enables the Servant to be God's light-filled covenant to both Jews and Gentiles (42:6). Light is an integral part of God's life-giving covenant (agreement). Those in need of God's help are pictured sitting in darkness (42:7); they dwell beneath the shadow of death (9:2). Their lives are characterized by gloom and distress (9:1) because they are walking (pursuing life's course) devoid of spiritual enlightenment. Jesus pointed out that a man will stumble when he walks by night (John 11:10). Ironically, owing to the insidious nature of sin, man loves the forces of his own destruction (John 3:19); conversely, he loathes that which is pure and undefiled. Apart from God's liberating intervention it is impossible for man to see the light of the gospel (2 Cor. 4:4). Like those addressed by Isaiah, he tragically sets darkness in the place of light (5:20). There has never been a time in history as now where man has more consistently set false notions in place of the true. Only futile thoughts and darkened foolish hearts remain when we exalt vain theories to the realm of truth (Rom. 1:21).

The Letter to the Hebrews declares the Messiah, God's Son, to be 'the radiance of God's glory' (1:3). He is, then, the source of light. God not only brings light; David says the Lord **is** his light (Ps. 27:1). Similarly, the One through whom God's covenant comes is, Himself, the very embodiment of that covenant. Isaiah's contemporary, Micah, said, 'This **One** shall be *shalom*' (wholeness – 5:5). In Him, the Lord really 'has become my salvation' (Isa. 12:2). The Servant-Messiah is God's covenant to the people (42:6). This is the reason why Matthew, when referring to Isaiah 42:4, emphasizes the fact that people will 'hope in His Name,' i.e., in the Messiah, Himself (Matt. 12:21). The quotation follows Jesus' healing of a man with a shriveled hand. Surely, it was no futile exercise to place one's hope in Him whose compassion embraced the entire spectrum of man's needs. It is evident that the Servant's heart is moved by man's awful plight: he comes to alleviate misery at its deepest and most personal level (42:7).

In Charles Wesley's beloved hymn, *And Can It Be*, we sing of God's flaming light filling our dungeon; that stanza concludes: 'My chains fell off, my heart was free, I rose, went forth, and followed Thee.' I know of no phrase that better expresses the essence of spiritual rebirth. How is this all accomplished? Paul says that the same sovereign Creator who said 'Let light shine out of darkness,' made His light shine in our hearts 'to give us knowledge of the glory of God...' (2 Cor. 4:6). As God breaks through our resistant spirit, He grants us the ability to trust in the light that He reveals to us. Jesus told His disciples that by trusting in the light they would become 'sons of light' (John 12:36), people whose way of life would stand in marked contrast to those who don't know where they're going (John 12:35). But while the Bible assumes that genuine believers will live their lives in concert with God's light, we are never permitted to take credit for whatever good we manage to do; 'We have this treasure in jars of clay to show that this all-surpassing power is from God and not from us' (2 Cor. 4:7).

It is God's pleasure to work through imperfect and weak vessels (even the broken reeds and smoldering wicks) that the glory may be rightly His alone.

Late in the chapter, Isaiah says, 'It pleased the LORD for the sake of His righteousness to make His law (or, teaching) great and glorious' (42:21). It is regrettably true that many who believe in the Light have a selective way of relating to His teaching. We seize upon certain truths (picking the ones which bring us comfort) while excluding those which (to borrow the prophet's words) take us 'along unfamiliar paths' (42:16). The true faith is no place for the spiritual dilettante.

The misery associated with man's dungeon-like existence stems from the fact that he has disregarded the light of life, God's written and living Word.

Rebellion brings with it 'gloom,' 'suffering,' and 'chains' (Psalm 107:10).

The Servant Songs call us to be people of God's Book. More specifically, we need to apply the teachings of His word to every aspect of our daily lives. Originally the term, fundamentalist, was used to describe someone who adhered to Scriptural fundamentals. Once people were called Methodists because they tried to incorporate the Bible's method into every life situation. But names aside, what matters most is that we're determined, by God's grace, to embrace the Scripture's values as our own. It's all too easy to hear the Word but not strive to put it into practice. The revivals of people like Wesley and Whitefield called for more than personal salvation. Wesley's ministry took him among the Kingswood coal miners where he took an open stand against their exploitation. Whitefield also called for the lifting of oppression in the workplace. Doing what's right identifies us as God's children; 'we must walk as Jesus did' (1 John 2:6). Let us therefore resolve to 'walk in the light, as He is in the light' (1 John 1:7). He who called His Son to a righteous cause (Isa. 42:6) has purposed for us to reflect the righteous light He has placed within us.

# 5

## Listen to Me ... Before I was born Yahweh called Me
*Isaiah 49:1-7*

Not everyone wanted to hear what the Servant had to say. To 'listen' (*sh'mah*) meant taking the message to heart. There is within us an inveterate stubbornness, an insensitivity to the things of God, an attitude well-known to Moses, the bringer of God's recurrent indictment against his people: 'They are a stiff-necked people indeed' (Deuteronomy 9:13). When Jesus preached His first sermon, Luke tells us that His message from Isaiah seemed to draw an initial response of appreciation; they were 'amazed at the gracious words that came from His lips' (Luke 4:22). Yet their approval turned to disdain when they recognized this well-spoken Rabbi as a former home-town resident, a member of a family they knew. Like them, we ever tend to be fascinated by externals; our understanding is dimmed by our failure to penetrate beyond that which attracts the eye. Machiavelli said, 'For the great majority of mankind are satisfied with appearances, as though they were realities, and are often more influenced by things that seem than by those that are.'[5] Isaiah (and the children God gave him [8:18]) pointed his people to beneath-the-surface reality.

As Isaiah's focus sharpens upon redemption's bedrock the rumblings of the Babylonian and Persian war machines are removed from center stage; they have receded into history and are no longer of concern to the prophet. For even the greatest kingdom conceived of by man appears but for a moment and is scattered by the wind. The 'mighty man' and all his work 'burn together, with no one to quench the fire' (1:31) – 'of what account is he?' (2:22). Scripture is preoccupied with that which abides: the never-ending kingdom of the Messiah (9:7). With Immanuel's reign in mind Isaiah is drawn still deeper into the truths of the Servant-Messiah's identity. In the ninth chapter the greatness of the miracle-child emerges as names such as 'Mighty God' and 'Everlasting Father' are ascribed to Him (9:6). We should not be at all surprised to learn of the Servant's consciousness of the eternal dimensions of His life's work. Like Jeremiah (1:4-5) and Paul (Galatians 1:15), His call to service was rooted in eternity. Unlike Jeremiah or Paul, the Messiah is the final Prophet, God's instrument of salvation for Israel and the Gentiles (Isaiah 49:6).

The Messiah heard His Father say, 'You are My Servant, Israel, in whom I will display My splendor' (49:3). It is clear that Isaiah is not referring to the nation (nor even a refined remnant), for the holy seed is no more than a stump in the land (6:13) out of which a tender but prolific shoot must yet spring forth (11:1). Most important, it is the nation that stands in need of God's restoration (49:5-6). Only One whose life perfectly reveals what God had intended 'Israel' to be – 'a holy people' (62:12) – has an inalienable right to the name. The Messiah's strength is in God who honors Him with approving testimony (49:5; Matt. 3:17). Through Him God displays His 'splendor,' a word conveying the idea of a 'bursting forth,' even of something splendid 'becoming visible.' The Scriptures reveal one dramatic event during Christ's three-year ministry when something of that splendor burst forth, on the Mount, where Jesus was briefly transfigured before three of His disciples and 'His face shone like the sun' (Matthew 17:2). What happened there was but a glimpse of an infinitely greater event: His eventual return to His world as the 'lifted up and highly exalted' Servant (52:13).

**Polished words**

The Servant's words are honed like a polished arrow (49:2), a shaft designed to penetrate the core of man's callous heart. The same heart which so desperately needs words of comfort (40:1) also needs to have its thoughts and attitudes judged and charged. Isaiah knows God to be both

Prosecutor and Advocate. And He has given us His word so that our heart's 'thoughts and attitudes' may be rightly evaluated (Heb. 4:12). In his novel, *Ethan Brand*, Nathaniel Hawthorne reaches the conclusion that the unforgivable sin is hardness of heart. From a scriptural standpoint, hardness of heart, while not the unforgivable sin, prevents us from taking the initiative to seek God. Each of us has a 'hard and unconverted heart' (Rom. 2:5); our heart's every inclination is 'only evil all the time' (Gen. 6:5). God must first enable us to inwardly hear His verdict of 'guilty!' ; it is a prerequisite if we are to cry out for grace. Simply stated, it is a matter of grace begetting grace.

Awareness of the superabundancy of God's grace is the antidote to despondency. There is no evidence that our Lord Jesus ever spoke the words, 'I have labored to no purpose and spent my strength in vain' (Isa. 49:4). But one may imagine Him being tempted in His humanity to respond like Jeremiah who poignantly articulated his pain in the face of his rejection, 'Why is my pain perpetual and my wound incurable.... Will You be to me like an unreliable stream' (Jer. 15:18)? Or we might think of Elijah when he cried, 'I have had enough, Lord; take my life' (1 Kings 19:4). Apparently there were those who were reminded of those prophets as they puzzled over Jesus' identity (Matt. 16:14).

There was a time when the crowds

accompanying Jesus began to thin out. We hear Jesus saying to the Twelve, 'Do you want to leave too' (John 6:67)?

Peter's immediate response on behalf of the disciples – 'to whom shall we go?' – reveals how effectively Jesus' words had influenced them. Jesus invited them to come after Him, and they did. As they spent time with the Master He made them think. What did the Law really say? What were the essentials in such weighty matters as righteousness and compassion? The disciples had to see truth from a new perspective. Jesus asked them to weigh the opinions of others and to reach scripturally-based conclusions. But He knew that coming up with the right answers required divine assistance (Matt. 16:17). This assistance God freely gave them. Through the ministry of the Spirit they recognized the Messiah's teaching to be words of eternal life (John 6:68), truth revealing God's splendor (6:69), for the Servant was both the Almighty's messenger and the message (Isa. 49:2-3).

The Servant-Messiah's confidence is again evident in His statement that the disciples remaining with Him were those whom Jesus had chosen (John 6:70); His work was to bring back the elect – the people kept safe by God (Isaiah 49:6). To that end, He is encouraged as He affirms, 'My reward (*peulla*, work) is with My God' (v. 5). Jesus always sought to do His work *coram Deo* (before the face of God); all that mattered to Him was His Father's approval. All who are committed to do God's work should, in a similar way, seek encouragement in the knowledge that the outcome of their labor – what is due them – is 'in the Lord's hand' (v. 4). The difficult situations we encounter are engineered by God so that we will seek His resources to deal with them. The process of becoming more like our Lord necessitates the growth of a more mature, resilient faith. Our intense trials compel us to reach out to Him who never allowed the hardships of life to diminish His trustful reliance upon His Father. Like our Savior, we need to have a settled hope in the provisions of God irrespective of our circumstances.

*'...what is due me is in the Lord's hand...'* (Isaiah 49:4)

Accolades do not always come to God's servants in this lifetime. Yet nothing in all of life – seen or unseen – is more satisfying than the soul's testimony that 'I am honored in the eyes of the Lord' (v. 5). I have heard many in God's service say that their life's choicest blessing will be to one day hear His words, 'Well done, good and faithful servant' (Matt. 25:21). Joseph Wittig said that a man's biography should really begin at his death rather than at birth; for it is at the termination of a man's life that his life's goals are revealed. May His grace cause us to be faithful

49

in those 'few things' (Matt. 25:21) that really matter and receive His approval on the day we stand before Him.

Isaiah refreshes us over and over again with the truth that God's prophetic word will not ultimately fail. It was in a Galatian synagogue, a place of considerable opposition to the gospel, that Paul and Barnabas turned to Isaiah 49:6 as they recognized God's plan to bring their Messiah's message to the Gentiles (Acts 13:47). Isaiah 49 broaches the mystery of Israel's hardening and reclamation. It is an important theme but one which is not given much exposition in the Servant Songs. Interested readers will find the theme prevalent in Romans 9-11 where much helpful insight may be found. Paul argues forcefully that it is inconceivable for God to cast off His elect (Rom. 11). Paul, himself, is an example of God's faithfulness to His own.

As a people, Israel has been put to one side for a time, but we have every reason to believe that God will, in the fulness of time, 'gather Israel again to Himself' (Isaiah 49:5) and make them holy indeed (62:12). Their rejection of the Messiah was all part of Heaven's plan and indirectly resulted in the spiritual enrichment of the Gentiles; their coming to know the Savior will bring even greater blessings to the nations (Rom. 11:12).

'It is a small thing,' Isaiah says, for the Servant 'to restore the tribes of Jacob...' (49:6). What is impossible for man – the changing of a human heart – is a 'small thing' for an omnipotent God. Some of us need to learn patience in the service of Heaven. Luke tells us that Jesus was in His Father's house at the age of twelve, in the initial stage of preparing for the ministry which was yet eighteen years away. Jesus was, as it were, hidden in His Father's quiver (49:2) for thirty years until God's timing was right for His appearance. God's timetable is always perfect. He says, 'I will answer you in the time of My favor' (49:8) – in a time when God finds it acceptable to do so. Here is a word for our time-bound, anxiety-prone hearts. God wants to set us free from the kind of nervousness which insists on quick answers and immediate resolutions. It was a lesson that virtually all the patriarchs and prophets had to learn. Paul expressed it this way:

> 'Therefore, my dear brothers, stand firm. Let nothing move you. Always give yourselves fully to the work of the Lord, because you know that your labor in the Lord is not in vain' (1 Cor. 15:58)

Hope bids us wait for a coming (perhaps imminent) day when all the true seed of Abraham will receive their promised inheritance. When Isaiah speaks of 'the day of salvation' (49:8) he has more in mind than Israel's release from her burdensome exile. No one summarizes the prophetic hope better than Isaiah: Heaven and earth rejoice as the desolate places are no longer barren and plentiful springs of water refresh the weary, afflicted ones; the difficult mountain trails become easy thoroughfares and the sun's heat no longer burns the traveler; God, Himself, compassionately guides those once held captive (49:9-13).

For Jesus' disciples, the Servant passages opened new dimensions to their understanding of the Messiah and His work, a perception radically different from anything they had ever heard. To them came the unsettling revelation concerning the insidious nature of sin and the terrible price their Master had willingly come to pay, not only for Israel's transgressions but also for the sin of the world.

Everything in this world is unstable and decaying. The legacy of empires founded on brute force is (or will eventually become) nothing but dust and ashes. We experience frustration as we gaze upon our society's perilous downward slide. Some years ago I came upon a clipped paragraph by American critic, Leslie Fiedler. His devastating analysis of the spirit of our age rings painfully true:

'We continue to insist that change is progress, self-indulgence is freedom and novelty is originality. In these circumstances it's difficult to avoid the conclusion that Western man has decided to abolish himself, creating his own boredom out of his own affluence, his own vulnerability out of his own strength, his own impotence out of his own erotomania, himself blowing the trumpet that brings the walls of his own city tumbling down. Having convinced himself that he is too numerous, he labors with pill and scalpel and syringe to make himself fewer, thereby delivering himself the sooner into the hands of his enemies. At last, having educated himself into imbecility and polluted and drugged himself into stupefaction, he keels over, a weary, battered old brontosaurus, and becomes extinct.'[5]

But man's folly is not the final word. Isaiah's name is a reminder of that fact, for it is derived from *yasha*, meaning 'to save.' Although the word often conveys the idea of military deliverance, Old Testament scholar Bruce Waltke noted a more subtle, 'legal' meaning as well. In one of his sermons on Psalms 3 and 4, he said: 'God delivers when it is morally right. Is it right that death should have the final word? Is it right that God's creation be consigned to irrevocable despair? If death and despair had the final word, then we would have to regard them as God.' How often the medical community strives heroically to enable the terminally ill to cling tenaciously to life for just a few extra days as if there were no hope beyond death's door. But we worship the living omnipotent God who 'will have compassion on His afflicted ones' (Isa. 49:13b); in the day He has chosen all of His redeemed creation will 'burst into song' (49:13a) and He who was rejected by

53

His own, once 'despised and abhorred' (49:7), will reign supreme. God says His Son 'will save His people from their sins' (Matt. 1:21); Jesus (*Yeshua*) is the perfect embodiment of the word *yasha*.

# 6

# The Sovereign Lord has opened My ears, and I have not been rebellious
### *Isaiah 50:4-9*

Since the *Ebhed* is one whose life is at the disposal of another, the life of the Servant is a disciplined life of obedience. What God is after is not perfunctory submission but, rather, heartfelt devotion to Him (Deut. 6:5). Up until the time of the Babylonian captivity, the most vexing problem facing Israel was idolatry. After centuries of warning, only radical discipline could stem the tide of evil in the nation. The Exile struck a decisive blow against the crass worship of the Baals. But Israel has not yet come into the fulness of God's plan for her, having rejected Him who came to give the world a living relationship with God (John 1:11). Her full salvation yet awaits them when their sins will be taken away (Rom. 11:25-27) and they, like Gentile believers, will no longer be bound over to disobedience (Rom. 11:30-32) but will be lovingly devoted to the Messiah.

Because of the Servant-Messiah's intimate relationship with His Father, He delighted in hearing His Father's words 'morning by morning' (Isa. 50:4) and never drew back from the obligations that the teaching placed upon Him, regardless of the consequences (5-6). Jesus understood well the relationship between law and love: obedience had to be the offshoot of one's devotion to God. Obedience must always be love's truest expression, manifesting itself tangibly, not just emotionally or with verbal superficiality (Matt. 7:21-22).

Learning to love the Father in ways acceptable to Him must be our primary concern, even as it was the all-consuming passion of the Servant. Jesus' disciples learned this by being with Him in close fellowship. When they finally went forth to serve God it was evident to those who observed them that the disciples had had an extended relationship with their Master (Acts 4:13). If we are to serve God well, we must also draw from our relationship with Him; everything springs from a vital connection with our Savior. This is nothing less than what Jesus specifically prayed for (John 17:20-23, 26).

By the time of His twelfth year, Jesus knew He must be in His Father's House. He was conscious of His need to learn for His own sake as well as for the sake of others. The Talmudic scholars believed that God would one day ask each Jew if he had set aside a regular time for study. Orthodox Judaism highly regards the dedicated study of the Torah and Talmud, even considering it a worthwhile, lifelong, exclusive vocation.

Learning was never simply obligatory for Jesus; He regarded the words of His Father to be of greater value than the food that sustained His physical life. (See John 4:31-34.)

It was typical in the Middle Eastern school of discipleship for the student to repeat the words of his teacher until they were recited *verbatim*. The Talmud (completed around AD 500) was largely the result of centuries of careful oral transmission of rabbinical teachings, from student to student, generation to generation (its *Mishneh*, containing the core of rabbinical legal requirements, comes from the word 'repetition'). Isaiah's allusion to this kind of painstaking process is evident; the Servant has been given 'the tongue of those who are taught' (50:4). The Servant-Messiah is the perfect disciple whose teachability is in no small way related to His undefiled spirit. Sin is the greatest obstacle to the acquisition of truth; the Messiah was born without that monstrous impediment (2 Cor. 5:21). This accounts for His deep insights which even in His youth caused men to marvel (Luke 2:47).

Messiah's listening unto obedience brought suffering and persecution (50:6). He embraced this destiny voluntarily, pursuing it with flint-like commitment (v. 7), giving His back to those who struck Him, His cheeks to those who plucked out the beard, and His face to mocking and spitting (v. 6).

The fullest sense of Isaiah's words were not

lost on Jesus, who resolutely set out for Jerusalem (Luke 9:51) knowing that He would be mocked, spat on, flogged, and killed (Mark 10:34). There is an unhurried deliberateness in the Messiah's work. We never see Him anxious about the outcome of His life's efforts. His calm pressing forward to embrace the Father's daily plan for His life, even with its painful realities, should inspire those who trust in Him to persevere with quiet confidence. For us, His past deliverances encourage us to hope in His present aid – even if our passageway descends into death's formidable valley.

While it remains for the final Servant Song (52:13-53:12) to delve more deeply into Messiah's suffering, His self-sacrifice is also prominent in Psalm 40:6-8 (which the NKJV translates):

> 'Sacrifice and offering You did not desire;
> My ears You have opened (or 'ears You have dug
> for me').
> Burnt offering and sin offering You did not require.
> Then I said, 'Behold, I come;
> In the scroll of the book it is written of me.
> I delight to do Your will, O my God...' '

When this text is quoted in Hebrews 10:5-7, the second line reads, '...a body You have prepared for Me.' Hebrews follows the Septuagint's (Greek Old Testament) translation of the verse which reveals the Messiah's willingness to offer Himself unto death. Although the text in the Hebrew Old Testament specifies the 'ears,' the meaning is

essentially the same in that it points to the
Messiah's attentiveness to His high calling's
demands. His ears having been awakened to the
need, He offers His body. Some have seen in the
'opened ear' of Psalm 40:6 an allusion to the
practice of boring the ear of a servant who so loved
his master that he willingly chose to be earmarked
as a faithful servant for life (Exod. 21:6). Jesus
dedicates Himself to His Father; the Son's ears
are attuned to the eternal plan; He holds back no
part of His life. He has learned of the inadequacy
of the Old Covenant sacrifices and is willing to
die once for all – the innocent in place of the guilty.

We marvel at the fathomless condescension
of the eternal God who, through His miraculous
birth (Isa. 7:14), became one of us. But beyond
this, the Servant-Messiah relinquished all personal
rights, submitting Himself to the indignities and
pain of the cross. Betrayed by a deceitful
mercenary, Jesus was sold for the price of a
common servant.

> Mine own Apostle, who the bag did bear,
> Though he had all I had, did not forbear
> To sell Me also and to put Me there
>  — Was ever grief like mine?
> For thirty pence he did my death devise,
> Who at three hundred did the ointment prize,
> Not half so sweet as my sweet sacrifice
> —Was ever grief like mine?
>
> George Herbert, *The Sacrifice*

We read of the legionnaries gambling for His seamless garment while bypassers jeered. Religious leaders speak of Him in the third person, 'He saved others, Himself He cannot save!' Robbers curse and taunt Him: 'Come down!' they say. All this He endures – and infinitely more – for us!

It is a fearful thing to suffer alone – to experience abandonment, especially in one's hour of deepest need. Messiah's cry of forsakenness in the midst of an impenetrable darkness compels us to ask, 'Why did He subject Himself to the horror of it all?' Isaiah tells us that the Servant was taught 'the word that sustains the weary' (50:4). It was through His own personal trauma that Jesus was able to offer that word, for it was by His death that He emptied death of its awful power (Heb. 2:15) and brought hope to a dying world. Jesus did more than tell people to follow after Him; He invited the weary and burdened to find their rest in Him (Matt. 11:28). His genuine offer is our only reliable solace in the midst of life's uncertainties and vicissitudes.

> The path we have to follow is a narrow one. It runs all the time on the edge of a precipitous mystery, sometimes taking you up to the sunlit heights and the Mountain of Transfiguration, and sometimes taking you down into the fires of suffering and into the shadow of death. Following Christ means that when you find these dizzy things before you, these dark things in your path, you go through them and not round them. Easy enough when the road runs by the

shining shores of the Lake of Galilee, but not so easy when it runs into the Garden of Gethsemane and becomes the *via dolorosa* ( L. P. Jacks,1860-1955).

For those who are weary in the race, Jesus' words ring with all the authority of Heaven; '[they] are spirit and they are life' (John 6:63).

We who have tasted His goodness have the privilege of being the Lord's blessing to others. God 'comforts us in all our troubles, so that we can comfort others with the comfort we ourselves have received from God' (2 Cor. 1:4).

Author Phillip Keller lived his childhood years in an unpleasant and discouraging boarding school. Yet his life was transformed by the influence of a little hunchbacked woman who radiated the comforting presence of Christ. She was the means through whom Jesus revealed His love for Phillip. Once Keller overheard her tell his parents that God would one day use him 'to achieve great things for His honor.' And the lad took confidence in the words of this simple, loving woman. To our fellow believers we are 'the aroma of Christ...the fragrance of life' (2 Cor. 2:15-16). We all need to be encouraged (Rom. 1:12), and there is no greater vehicle for the expression of encouragement than our speech. Paul exhorts us to speak 'only what is helpful for building up others according to their needs, that it may benefit those who listen' (Eph. 4:29). Failure to strive to bring God's word of comfort to the needy is, at heart, a failure of love. With great sorrow we must confess that many who identify themselves as Christians have effectively denied their Lord by using their tongues as destructive instruments. Their words deny life to the weary. Evangeline Paterson wrote plaintively concerning them:

Weep, weep for those
Who do the work of the Lord
With a high look
And a proud heart.
Their voice is lifted up
In the streets, and their cry is heard.
The bruised reed they break
By their great strength, and the smoking flax
They trample.

Weep not for the quenched
(For their God will hear their cry
 And the Lord will come to save them)
But weep for the quenchers

For when the Day of the Lord
Is come, and the vales sing
And the hills clap their hands
And the light shines

Then shall their eyes be opened
On a waste place,
Smouldering,
The smoke of the flax bitter
In their nostrils,
Their feet pierced
By broken reed-stems...

Wood, hay, and stubble,
And no grass springing,
And all the birds flown.

Weep, weep for those
Who have made a desert
In the name of the Lord. [6]

## Unflagging hope

The Servant's confidence in His vindication is the theme of Isaiah 50:7-9.

'He is near who justifies Me' (50:8) must be understood within the context of a court of law. Charges are brought against the Servant but the accusations are false and will not come to rest upon God's chosen one, whose support comes from Heaven (v. 7). 'Who is My accuser? Let him confront Me' (v. 8), is reminiscent of Jesus' challenge to His detractors: 'Can any of you prove Me guilty of sin' (John 8:46)? It is dangerous to ask your enemies to point out your faults unless, of course, you've led an entirely blameless life.

Men may scorn and ridicule Him but their mockery cannot last. Unlike His adversaries who all wear out like a moth-eaten garment (50:9), the Servant will neither perish nor decay. Overtones of His deity are implicit within the verse. The confidence He expresses, 'I know I will not be put to shame' (v. 7), is the assurance He conveys to all who trust in Him. Paul, who once sought to justify himself through legalistic obedience, rejoices in Isaiah's revelation. Note how the ex-

Pharisee is moved by the spirit of the Servant's question, 'Who is he that will condemn me?' (v. 9), when he says, 'Who will bring any charge against those whom God has chosen?' (Rom. 8:33). The query is rhetorical. 'It is God who justifies.' Who could possibly condemn us?

There is nothing more remarkable (or perhaps more difficult to comprehend) than the fact that God has purposed to justify all 'those who have faith in Jesus' (Rom. 3:26). Nothing is more difficult for the very religious to comprehend than that God should justify the wicked. But for the wicked (you and me), grace means everything. It has been rightly said that unless grace means everything it means nothing at all. Were it not for God's sovereignly given grace, 'darkness,' 'gloom' and 'distress' would perpetually describe our sorry state (Isa. 9:1-2).

Chapter 50's final verses present two options for 'him who walks in the dark' (v. 10). By God's grace he may obey the word spoken by the Servant; obedience to that word will be expressed in trusting and relying on his God. Divine 'economics' declares that the death of the Messiah in the place of sinners justifies (makes righteous before God) all who trust in the merits of His sacrifice for them. They recognize they are powerlessness to save themselves and find help solely in the fact that 'Christ died for the ungodly' (Rom. 5:6).

But another image looms before us. It is the pathetic sight of people who are existing with only the slightest illumination yet who are trying to walk in the light of their little fires (50:11). They prefer their self-generated sparks to the light of the Messiah. Here are those who trust in their own resources in spite of the immeasurable grief awaiting them. When America was faced with powerful wartime enemies, President Roosevelt told the nation that there was nothing to fear but fear itself. While there was timely practical wisdom in what he said, to a prudent view of all the evidence must be added this caveat: 'It is a fearful thing to fall into the hands of the living God' (Heb. 10:31). To all who are bent on pursuing an independent course, God speaks a warning tinged with irony: 'Go, walk in the light of your fires and of the torches you have set ablaze. This is what you shall receive from My hand: You will lie down in torment' (50:11).

It cannot be denied that sometimes the child of God finds himself walking in the dark (50:10). When Dante begins his classic, *Inferno*, he finds himself in dark woods with a foreboding sense that his own soul is in jeopardy. We have all known what it is to lose our orientation in life – to feel that all is dark about us. Isaiah exhorts God's people not to lose confidence in their sovereign God. We must not doubt in the darkness what God has revealed to us in the light.

Our tendency is to try to call upon whatever reserves of faith we can muster when we are confronted by a crisis. Yet we often fail to trust God in the everyday occurrences of life, forgetting that God wants us to trust Him in the 'little' matters, what might be thought of as our mundane, ordinary circumstances. An Anglican minister of a former generation told his people:

> 'Let our trust be reared in the humble nursery of our own daily experience, with its ever recurring little wants, and trials, and sorrows; and then, when need be, it will come forth, to do such great things as are required of it' (Philip Power, *The 'I wills' of the Psalms*).

There was never a time when the Servant of the Lord failed to trust in His heavenly Father's provisions. Let us learn from Him to keep our hopes fixed upon God regardless of our situation or the extent of our need. Isaiah assures us that our Savior is a precious, sure foundation; the one who trusts in Him will never be dismayed (28:16). As we look back upon our brief lives as believers we will be hard-pressed to find a time when God was not totally faithful. His grace which was sufficient to bring us through our many past crises will never fail us — even when we must 'pass through the rivers' and 'walk through the fires' of life (43:2).

# 7

# Behold, My Servant
*Isaiah 52:13-15*

Isaiah 52:13-15 is the first of five stanzas (each with three verses) which together comprise the largest, climactic section on the Servant (52:13-53:12). It is set appropriately at the center of Isaiah's Book of Consolation (40–66). A massive two-volume compilation of ancient and modern rabbi-nic thought on this portion of Isaiah by Jewish Orthodoxy (*Isaiah 53 According to the Rabbis* – KTAV Publishing) fails to reach any firm decision regarding the identity of the servant. Rashi, a prolific expositor and highly regarded eleventh century French Jewish scholar, consist-ently main-tained that Isaiah's Servant was the nation of Israel, a position that the venerable Maimonedes believed was untenable. As one reads the opinions of these well-meaning scholars it is like a breath of fresh air to study an event which involved a first century believer named Philip and a foreigner who had been worshiping in Jerusalem. Luke tells us that Philip approached the chariot of an Ethiopian eunuch who, after the ancient fashion, was reading aloud from the Scriptures. Philip asked him if he understood what he was reading (Acts 8:30). The man responded, 'How can I, unless someone explains it to me?' (verse 31). The text in question, Isaiah 53:7-8, is concerned with the sufferings of the Servant, comparing Him to a lamb who had been unjustly slaughtered.

> The eunuch asked Philip, 'Tell me, please, who is the prophet speaking about, himself or someone else?' Then Philip began with that very passage of Scripture and told him the good news about Jesus (Acts 8:34-35).

The straightforward account in Acts should make us aware of how very much we are dependent upon God's help – His revelation – if we are to interpret His Word accurately. Although the Jewish community has traditionally thought of this final Servant Song in messianic terms,[7] how wonderful it will be in that day when multitudes of the household of Israel accept the Scripture's reliable witness through such men as Luke and Philip. The fact remains that the final Song's fifteen verses fit none other so well as the Messiah as He was revealed in first century Palestine; if they do not refer to Jesus, we do not have the remotest idea of whom Isaiah was speaking.

We recall that in the fortieth chapter Isaiah began his God-given message of comfort, assuring the people that their sin had been paid for, their hard service ended. He spoke words of hope to the heart of a downcast nation: God would pass through the devastated wastelands of their lives, restoring the bruised and fallen, even transforming them into a highway for the manifestation of His presence in the world. The sure foundation for every aspect of God's consolation is the well-developed subject of the final Song.

## The chief question

The question which must invariably be asked concerning any servant is, 'Did he do the work he was sent to do?' There is no doubt that Jesus understood and undertook to do His Father's will. As His days on the earth drew to a close He prayed to His Father, 'I have brought You glory on earth by completing the work You gave Me to do' (John 17:4). Isaiah's panoramic vision of the outworking of that will is now explored for us in-depth.

There is no hesitancy on the part of Isaiah to assure the reader of the Servant's successful service. He begins by proclaiming the Messiah's triumph, a victory which is linked to His wise (or prudent) dealings (52:13). To 'act wisely' (*shakal*) combines the ideas of wise action with the successful outcome of those actions. As Jeremiah later watched the collapse of Jewish society he prophesied of the wise reign of the Messiah who would do what was right for the sake of Israel (Jer. 23:5). His greatness would be bound up with the name ascribed to Him, *Yahweh Tzidkenu*, 'The

Lord our righteousness' (Jer. 23:6). His wise course of action would bring salvation to His people. In such promises, 'righteousness' and 'salvation' are virtually synonymous: to have God's righteousness is to have His salvation. The key point to bear in mind is that God's righteousness comes to us through His Servant: *He* is our righteousness. This is the very heart of the gospel: because of His successful ministry as the Servant of the Lord He has become 'our righteousness, holiness, and redemption' (1 Cor. 1:30). The Law holds out life to the obedient (Lev. 18:5) but brings nothing to enable us to perfectly comply with its extensive demands. The gospel tells us in whom we may trust and brings God's life-changing power.

The Messiah's victory stems from His vindication. He declared that He would not be disgraced but, rather, honored in the eyes of His God (50:7; 49:5). The unparalleled honor bestowed upon Him marks both the beginning (52:13) and the conclusion of this fourth Song (53:12). Commenting on the thirteenth verse, a Talmudic *Midrash* (commentary) says of Isaiah's Servant, 'He shall be exalted above Abraham, lifted up above Moses, and be higher than the ministering angels.' That interpretation reveals a sensitivity to the sequential character of the conjunctions, one event following logically on the heels of another: 'raised *and* lifted up *and* highly exalted.'

If we view the prophecy through the lens of history it is not going too far afield to see the anticipated glory bursting forth in Jesus' resurrection ('raised up'), ascension ('lifted up'), and being seated at the Father's right hand ('highly exalted'). Through that ultimate triumph, God's light and peace will be manifested to the nations (Isaiah 49:6; Micah 5:5).

Yet having announced the Servant's glorification, we are immediately returned to the school of suffering and are confronted again with one who, though despised (49:7), did not hide Himself from beatings, shame and spitting (50:6). And the picture becomes even more graphic: 'His appearance was so disfigured beyond that of any man and His form marred beyond human likeness' (52:14). Isaiah uses the word, *shamem*, which conveys an image so horrifying that people who see Him are left speechless.

When Israel's Prime Minister, Yitzhak Rabin, was assassinated many were dumbstruck by the unconscionable fact that a fellow Jew was his murderer. The brute reality of the death of a man who so valued peace left many bewildered. When Jesus' countrymen sought and achieved His death, it was also an occasion for bewilderment and downcast faces (Luke 24:17). Nonetheless, beneath the surface of the Messiah's gross indignities, something phenomenal was taking place: God was ushering in the covenant of which

Jeremiah and Ezekiel spoke six hundred years earlier (Chapters 31 and 36, respectively).

In an upper room on the evening of the observance of Passover (the commemoration of a deliverance made possible by the shed blood of spotless lambs) the Servant of the Lord raises a cup of wine and says, 'This is My blood of the covenant, which is poured out for many' (Mark 14:24). The Servant is bringing God's salvation to the world – He is about to 'sprinkle' many nations (Isaiah 52:15).

The word translated 'sprinkle', *naza*, occurs some two dozen times in the Old Testament. Curiously, the Revised Standard Version renders it 'sprinkle' in all but two of those references: here, where it is translated 'startle,' and in 2 Kings 9:33 ('spattered'). Apparently, the RSV translators had a difficult time making sense out of the act of sprinkling, a deed both understood and deeply appreciated by those who have known the cleansing work of their Lord. The apostle Peter's first letter opens with the acknowledgment of the sprinkling of the Messiah's blood as the avenue of God's abundant grace and peace (1 Pet. 1:2). The Scriptures anticipate many – even those of high rank – gratefully responding to this work of God in His Servant. Isaiah foresees kings shutting their mouths because of what is revealed to them (Isa. 52:15). In their silence they are given grace to understand the significance of what the Servant has accomplished. They are among those whose spiritual perception has been radically altered as they've been confronted with 'the foolishness and weakness of God' (1 Cor. 1:25). We are again given cause to reflect upon the wonder of His grace which enlightens all classes of people.

Primarily, the sprinkling of blood advertises the death of a victim. As such it draws from the Old Testament's sacrificial ritual of cleansing. In that context none carries greater significance than Moses' sprinkling the people with sacrificial blood when God's covenant was ratified with them at Mount Sinai: 'Moses ... took the blood, sprinkled it on the people, and said, "This is the blood of the covenant that the LORD has made with you in accordance with all these words" '(Exod. 24:8). 'All these words', of course, refer essentially to the commandments representing the heart and soul of God's *b'rit*, or contractual agreement, with His people. For many centuries afterwards, the people forsook God by neglecting or spurning the laws of His covenant. Like virtually all of Israel's prophets, Isaiah was commissioned to proclaim God's word to a people whose heart had become obdurate and whose eyes were closed to their holy God's message (6:9-10). But although they provoked His judgment, God assured them that He had not utterly forsaken them. Blood sprinkled upon the altar and the people was designed to show that justice had been tempered by mercy.

It is not uncommon to hear Jewish comment-ators speak of the Torah as the marriage *b'rit* that binds Yahweh, Israel's husband, to Israel, His bride. Yet it is not the Law which binds God to the nation. It is, and has always been, grace. In Isaiah 55:3 God identifies His eternal covenant with Israel as 'the faithful mercies of David.' It is God's covenantal faithfulness upon which Israel's relationship with their Savior rests. Even more wonderful than God's love itself is His extra-ordinary persistence in it. Though we be faithless, like the prophet Hosea's wife, yet does God love us; He will yet reclaim and purify His sin-defiled bride.

In one of the Old Testament's brightest moments, Jeremiah (who suffered terrible indignities for serving God faithfully) received the word of the Lord promising to eventually establish a new covenant with His people (31:31-34). Jeremiah anticipates two remarkable features flowing from that covenant: the writing of God's *torah* (law) upon man's heart (rather than on stone tablets) and a far-reaching forgiveness of sin reminiscent of David's joyful realization in Psalm 103:12: 'As far as the east is from the west, so far has He removed our transgressions from us.'

The first of the new covenant blessings brings intimate fellowship with God (individuals will 'know' Him); the second part of the agreement's blessing (the forgiveness of sin) actually makes

74

possible the first: 'They will all know Me ... for I will forgive their iniquity...' (31:34). The genuine imprint of true religion, Jeremiah teaches, is not the offshoot of such admonitions as 'know the Lord!' (verse 34a) but is the result of one's inner experience of God's freely bestowed forgiveness.

In a parallel prophecy, Ezekiel assures God's covenant people that the Lord, Himself, will cleanse them, sprinkling them, as it were, with pure water (36:25). God does the work sovereignly. We are not unlike Abraham in Genesis 15 who, while Yahweh passed between the pieces of slain animals, sat off to the side receiving God's covenantal blessings. The Lord does not change His mind about the recipients of His love and will never permit us to be separated from the Messiah's love (Rom. 8:35-39). To put it another way: God hates divorce (Mal. 2:16); He has married His people for better or for worse.

Two Hebrew words, often used in the context of marriage, may help us better understand the depths of God's commitment to us. There is a general love (*ahabah*), which launches a marriage. It is profound in itself. But it is *chesed*, a gracious and faithful loving-kindness, that sustains the relationship over time. It is that love – 'the *chesed* given to David' – in which Isaiah particularly delights (55:3). Earlier in the chapter where Jeremiah announces the promise of the new covenant, he employs both Hebrew words that

God's people might be encouraged to rest securely in His grace: 'I have loved you with an everlasting love (*ahabah*); therefore I have continued to love (*chesed*) you' (Jer. 31:3). These are words for us to live by – a divine pledge of God's surging, passionate love in sunshine or shadow.

'Though the mountains be shaken and the hills be removed, yet my faithful, covenant love for you will not be shaken' (Isa. 54:10).

# 8

## Who has believed our message?
*Isaiah 53:1-3*

God's grace exceeds human imagination. His thoughts are not our thoughts (Isa. 55:8), especially in matters pertaining to our salvation.

In fact, they run quite contrary to our expectations. I once read aloud from the 53rd chapter of Isaiah while praying over a sick Jewish child. His mother offered a mild protest and asked me if I wouldn't mind also reading something from the *Tenak* (the Old Testament). Her ignorance concerning the contents of that chapter was no great surprise to me; long ago the synagogue deleted it from its regularly scheduled readings from the *Haphtorah* (the prophets). It points us to the cross whose message seems so out of character for God. The Muslim's *Quran* denies the crucifixion of Jesus ('*Isa*) altogether. Islamic theology cannot brook the thought of God allowing such an ignominious end for a prophet. As an imam (Muslim leader) told me, 'God would not allow His righteous servant to suffer so.'

Physical blemish disqualified a person for the priesthood; no one who had any sort of defect could approach God's altar of sacrifice (Lev. 21).

Doubtless the same restriction was also applicable to Israel's kings. But here is a Priest-King who has suffered so badly – He scarcely seems human – that we instinctively turn away. 'Who would have believed what we have heard' (53:1)? Unbelief is caused by revulsion as well as by the fact that God is doing something beyond our powers of comprehension.

Simplicity characterized the Servant's life as well as His appearance. There was nothing externally impressive attracting people to this 'tender shoot,' this 'root out of dry ground' (53:2). Isaiah had compared the nation to a veritably lifeless stump (11:1) out of which the messianic Branch would appear. While growing up in Nazareth (not at all as charming a place as Sunday school lessons may have suggested) He was unrecognized by His peers. His family members thought Him mad. Even Peter, who was the first apostle to gain insight into Jesus' Messiahship, did not confess Him as such until after two full years of intimate fellowship.

At the same time, Isaiah knew that the salvation in which he rejoiced would be revealed on a large scale. Immediately preceding the fourth Song he wrote, 'The LORD will lay bare His holy arm in the sight of all the nations, and all the ends of the earth will see the salvation of our God' (52:10). The Servant's love for all nations is evident in the sweeping statement: 'Blessed be Egypt, my people, and Assyria, the work of My hands, and Israel, mine inheritance' (19:25). Although the Messiah surely came to 'give His life a ransom for many' (Mark 10:45), Isaiah asks, 'To whom has the arm of the LORD been revealed' (53:1)?

The prophet knows all along that the message of the Servant's salvation will be met by those who say, 'This is so much folly,' like those who contemptuously appear to mimic the prophet's speech: '*sav lasav sav lasav...*' (28:13). But there will be those who say, 'This is worthy of faith.' Whenever this positive conclusion is held the believer has cause to identify with Peter by recognizing his enlightenment unto faith as a gift of divine origin (Matthew 16:17; cf. Ephesians 2:8).

### 'Glory to the Righteous One' (Isa. 24:16)
We hear songs coming from the ends of the earth in praise of His Name. Who, then, is this Servant-Messiah?

In an earlier Song, the Servant says that before He was called, the Lord made mention of His name (49:1). In the seventh chapter of Isaiah, the Servant is called *Immanuel* ('God with us') and His birth deemed supernatural (7:14). Scholars have long argued over the meaning of the word *almah*, some insisting that it does not necessarily mean 'virgin.' While the criticism is not without its merits (*almah* need not always designate a virgin), it is never used in Scripture to identify a married woman. Moreover, we may reasonably assume (understanding Israelite culture) that Isaiah's listeners would normally consider an unmarried female Israelite to be a virgin. But linguistic considerations aside, Isaiah speaks of a particular pregnancy and birth as 'a sign' from God (7:14). That in itself cries out for an extraordinary event (it is hard to imagine how an ordinary birth would be recognised as 'a sign'). We believe that Isaiah's words refer to the same person whose birth in Bethlehem was prophesied by his contemporary, Micah, who referred to the Messiah as One 'whose origin is from old, from everlasting' (Mic. 5:2).

It is true that Isaiah's prophecy seems to anticipate an imminent birth (7:16). It is not unreasonable to suggest that the verse found a partial fulfilment in the birth of Isaiah's son (8:3-4) while nonetheless looking forward to the wondrous birth of Him whose name would be called 'Wonderful Counselor, Mighty God, Everlasting Father, Prince of Peace' (9:6). The 'Son' of 7:14 and 9:6 is one and the same, whose royal titles at once convey both His humanity and deity.

## Prophecies about the Servant-Messiah (52:13-53:12)

*Prophecies Fulfilled\**

| | |
|---|---|
| His exaltation (52:13): | Philippians 2:9; Hebrews 1:3 |
| His disfigurement (52:14): | Mark 15:15, 17, 19 |
| His rejection (53:1, 3): | John 12: 37-40 |
| His burden-bearing (53:4): | Matthew 8:16-17; 1 Peter 2:24 |
| His blood sacrifice (53:5): | Romans 3:25; 1 Peter 1:18-19 |
| His death for sinners (53:6, 8): | 2 Corinthians 5:21; Hebrews 9:28 |
| His voluntary death (53:7): | John 10:11, 18 |
| His burial (53:9): | John 19:38-42 |
| His justifying work (53:10, 11): | Romans 5:18-19; Hebrews 10:14 |
| His death with sinners (53:12): | Mark 15:27; Luke 22:37 |
| His sharing His 'spoils' (53:12a): | Hebrews 9:15; Revelation 7:15-17 |

## A selective unveiling

'To whom has the arm of the LORD been revealed' (53:1)?

John says Isaiah saw Jesus' glory and spoke about Him (John 12:41). Curiously, John mentions Isaiah's vision of the Messiah immediately after

---

\*The Scriptures cited are only representative of the New Testament texts relating to the fulfilment of Isaiah's prophecies. There is also, of course, an overlap, even repetition, of themes in some of the verses mentioned.

the remarks that God 'blinded the people's eyes and deadened their hearts,' preventing them from believing the message. John's reference is to Isaiah 6:10 where God tells Isaiah of the frustration he will experience in bringing His word to Israel. The opening verses of Isaiah 53 confirm this in a nutshell: Israel placed no value on the Messiah; they 'esteemed Him not' (53:3).

More than seven centuries later the apostle Paul would tell all entrusted with the gospel message that to some they'd be 'the fragrance of life,' to others 'the smell of death' (2 Cor. 2:16). Only an accurate perception of the ineffable greatness of their Savior would enable them to persevere in the midst of rejection and persecution. Sometimes, like Isaiah, we will be pressed to savor His presence (even something of His glory) in an unresponsive, inhospitable climate. Bonhoeffer (who was executed by the Nazis) taught his fellow believers not to be surprised when they faced suffering; in fact, he told them to receive it with joy as a token of God's grace.

Someone has said, 'You cannot show at the same time that Christ is wonderful and you are clever.' Our Lord Jesus never tried to cleverly argue people into the kingdom of God. Like Him, our task in every situation is to speak God's word and leave the results entirely with Him. Mother Teresa was right when she said, 'God has not called me to be successful; He has called me to be faithful.' It is no small comfort to know that even when rejection comes, the King of kings is still completely in charge.

Having known the heartbreak of rejection, I realize how difficult it is to continue to love those who have rejected me. To maintain an attitude of love for them requires supernatural aid. A profound stimulus may be found in taking to heart the fact that our Savior did not reject those who despised Him.

He returned blessings for insults.

### 'Amazing love, how can it be...?'

'God dying for man,' said theologian P.T. Forsyth. 'I am not afraid of that phrase; I cannot do without it.'[8] If the Messiah were only a man, or some superman, there are insuperable problems facing those who would trust Him as their Savior.

If we deny that Jesus was also God revealed in the flesh then He must be viewed as an independent third party in the drama of redemption. With respect to the biblical concept of substitutionary atonement (e.g., Rom. 5:8), how would it be possible (or morally tenable) for a human being to stand in the place of others and receive the punishment due them? Even if our substitute were sinless, would he not be cast in the role of a victim set apart to placate the wrath of a remote and angry God? Would it not ring of Shakespeare's Venetian 'Merchant' demanding his 'pound of flesh?' More to the point, would the idea of grace have any leg upon which to stand? If grace speaks of the *unmerited* forgiveness of God, must we not insist that God, Himself, pay the penalty due us for our transgressions? Must not God satisfy the demands of His own holy love by dying in our place? Is that not essential in order for God to be just as well as the justifier of the one who has faith in Jesus (Rom. 3:26)?

Because of His holiness it was impossible for God to be indifferent concerning human sin. He had to either inflict punishment for it or bear it, Himself. Because He chose to do the latter, we may speak gladly of His grace, for God's own body was shattered on the cross for our sins. I have heard of an Italian art gallery displaying a painting of the crucifixion in which the spear thrust through the Savior penetrates a shadowy figure in the background. It was the artist's way of dealing with the mystery of the Father's suffering: God's own heart was pierced and broken on the accursed tree; He was indeed in Christ reconciling the world to Himself (2 Cor. 5:19). We are confronted with the greatest of mysteries; for Jesus, Himself, is no less Divine. He took up the sacred name of *Yahweh* (John 8:58) in concert with Isaiah's prophetic announcement: He shall be called *El Gibbor*, 'Mighty God' (9:6). But the deity of Christ can only be fully attested to by those who are in covenant with Him; it is our pardon in Him and the evangelical experience of it that forms the basis for our convictions every bit as much as a clear understanding of the written Gospel.[9]

From a deeply personal perspective, John Stott has insightfully written:

'I could never believe in God, if it were not for the cross.... In the real world of pain, how could one worship a God who was immune to it?... He laid aside his immunity to pain.... He suffered for us. Our sufferings become more manageable in the light of His. There is still a question mark against human suffering, but over it we boldly stamp another mark, the cross, which symbolizes divine suffering.'[10]

Suffering's brute reality has made it difficult for many people to believe in a loving, compassionate God. As one survivor of the *holocaust* (lit., 'burnt offering') exclaimed, 'After Auschwitz it is impossible to believe in God.'

Pulitzer prize author, Elie Wiesel, whose family perished in the Nazi death camps, did not deny God's existence, only His justice. Those who believe in a God who is detached from the cause and effect of suffering have not seriously contemplated the Scripture's teaching on the subject: 'I form the light and create darkness, I bring prosperity and create disaster' (Isa. 45:7, cf. Exod. 4:11). There is much perplexing about affliction, as Paul, himself, straightforwardly declares (2 Cor. 4:8). It is not unspiritual for us to say we simply do not understand why certain events (including our own griefs) are allowed to occur. In distressful times the Bible may appear to be a 'problem' book as much as an 'answer' book; darkness may seem to be one's closest friend (Ps. 88:18).

Our bewilderment notwithstanding, we must never lose track of the fact that God, Himself, has experienced the whole spectrum of human suffering. He personally knows what it is to suffer (Heb. 4:15), by which we may draw some measure of consolation. Isaiah says, 'In all their distress He too was distressed' (63:9). Jesus took a man's heart back to heaven so that He might be a truly compassionate High Priest. When we struggle, as we invariably must with what appears to be the free range of evil, the cross quiets our troubled souls. 'It is,' as Forsyth said, 'God's only self-justification in such a world' as this.[11]

Although Isaiah knew great sorrow and persecution, himself, he was encouraged by his vision of the Holy One of Israel made sin for him and by the hope capsulized in God's promise that one day, 'The redeemed ... will enter Zion with singing; everlasting joy will crown their heads. Gladness and joy will overtake them, and sorrow and sighing will flee away' (35:10). For Isaiah, the future dominates the present; his thoughts of what must be undergird him in a world of unremitting turmoil. The Servant is none other than the Davidic Messiah, the indisputable Lord of history.

When Isaiah saw 'the King, the Lord Almighty' (6:5), he entered into the presence of Him whose altar atoned for the prophet's sin (6:7). Isaiah had the distinct privilege of entering into God's presence even though he knew himself to be sinful. He was still a sinner when he communed with the Almighty; God's altar made all the difference, providing Isaiah with the gift of holiness. The prophet is a type of each true believer who is, in the same moment and throughout his life, both sinner and saint.

No chapter in all of the Old Testament helps us better understand the Messiah's vicarious, atoning work than Isaiah's 53rd chapter. As we continue to read it, may we not lose sight of Him and the holy ground upon which we stand.

**9**

# Truly He took up our infirmities
*Isaiah 53:4-6*

Much of the Servant's work is couched in what is called 'the prophetic perfect,' a way of Hebraic writing which describes a future event as if it has already happened. We are repeatedly pressed to acknowledge the fact that the cross was not a divine afterthought, that even at the moment of our first parents' disobedience God announced His plan to bruise the Messiah's heel to free mankind from its pollution and guilt (Gen. 3:15).

The nature of messianic prophecy is progressive; each prophecy casts more light on the subject. This occurs, for example, respecting the concept of the 'seed': Messiah is to be born of a woman (Gen. 3:15), through the line of Shem (9:26) and specifically through Abraham (22:18). Yet even as late as Genesis 22:18, the 'seed' is not clearly presented as a person, since *zerah* (seed) may indicate a singular or plural object. Still less apparent in these early stages of messianic prophecy is the nature of the 'bruising' which is to occur. Yet the idea of the Messiah being crushed for sin is implicit in the Genesis pronouncement as is the violence associated with

88

that act. The verb *shuph* (to bruise) occurs in rabbinic commentaries describing Moses 'grinding' the golden calf until it was fine powder (Exod. 32:20). It remains for Isaiah (along with David in Psalm 22) to portray the depths of the Servant's suffering.

Matthew quotes Isaiah 53:4: 'Ours were the sicknesses that He bore' (Matt. 8:17). The Hebrew language does not distinguish between the sources of illness but Isaiah says He carried our pains: He was stricken, smitten, afflicted, pierced, and crushed (53:4-5). Some Talmudic writers have recognized the likelihood that suffering is bound up with Messiah's work.[12] Among the ancient prayers said for the Day of Atonement may be found the words of Eleazar ben Qalir (perhaps as late as AD 1000): 'Our righteous Messiah has departed from us; we are horror-stricken, and there is none to justify us. Our iniquities and the yoke of our transgressions he carries, and is wounded for our transgressions. He bears on his shoulders our sins to find pardon for our iniquities.' Another rabbi, Eliyya de Vidas, was thinking in a similar vein when he said: 'It follows that whosoever will not admit the Messiah thus suffers for our iniquities must endure and suffer them for himself.'

However, these statements are atypical of the general response of Israel. Those for whom He offered Himself misunderstood His death entirely, thinking that He was 'stricken by God' for some evil He had committed (53:4). But what Jesus did was to bring us a salvation as deep and as wide as our sin. Matthew points to Jesus as the fulfilment of Isaiah's messianic hope following a series of healings: a centurion's paralyzed servant, Peter's fever-ridden mother-in-law, and many who were demon-possessed. Matthew says that the Savior 'drove out the spirits with a word and healed all the sick' (8:16). Isaiah prophesied of a day when the eyes of the blind would be opened, the ears of the deaf unstopped, and the lame leap like a deer (35:5-6). All this and more gave evidential support to the inbreaking of God's kingdom (Matt. 11:5), the first fruits of a coming day when weakness and decay would finally be consigned to the forgotten past. The blessings of that day are too profound for even the most sanctified minds to imagine (1 Cor. 2:9). Of one thing we may be certain. Its underlying truth is not limited to the remote future: God intervenes – He acts – on behalf of those who habitually wait for Him (Isa. 64:4).

## Our cleansing complete

Jesus did something no self-respecting rabbi of His day would ever do: He laid His hands on the sick. Contact with the diseased drew ceremonial defilement. It was not the task of a rabbi to heal the sick. Neither did the Levitical priest have this function. His role was that of an inspector: he would examine an individual, once sick, when it was thought that he was restored to health and able to re-enter Jewish society. (See Luke 17:14.)

The Gospel narratives reveal a Messiah who decisively and dramatically shows that He has the cure for all that ails and destroys us. And His healing came to us not by His all-powerful word, but by His taking the essence of our sickness to Himself. For sin is the root of all affliction. Jesus, the flawless Servant, took the very heart of our sickness upon Himself. There is a sense in which He touched the diseased fully intending to become defiled.

A reading of the Gospels reveals a compassionate Savior who is very much concerned with the needs of the body. Inasmuch as He is forever the same, we should not be reluctant to look to Him for relief and healing when we, ourselves, are afflicted. Joachim Neander's hymn speaks well for us all: '...How oft in grief hath not He brought thee relief, spreading His wings to o'ershade thee!'

Yet although 'ours were the sicknesses He bore,' it is not Isaiah's intention for us to conclude that it is invariably God's will to restore the physical well-being of His people. We know, for example, that the apostle Paul was afflicted with an ailment that God chose not to remove. Although Paul was weakened as a result, the physical hardship only made him rely upon his

Savior all the more. Through that reliance he experienced God's power in a vital way. In fact Paul even learned to delight in his weaknesses, seeing them as an indirect vehicle for the manifestation of God's strength (2 Cor. 12:10) and opportunity for service, too, as he reminds the church: 'It was because of an illness that I first preached the gospel to you' (Gal. 4:13). As far as our current physical state is concerned, we must ultimately bow to the sovereign will of Him whose will is often inscrutable but who has promised that He will one day give us a new and flawless body like that of our resurrected and glorified Lord (Phil. 3:21).

The Bible presents Jesus' healing miracles not only as evidence of His compassion for our physical distress but also as signs clearly affirming His Messiahship. His miracles are never presented merely as wonders, *per se*. This is especially true in John's Gospel where the profusion of Christ's healings consistently point to His identity and reveal the restorative power with which the Messiah is invested.

Hebrew has several words which help explain our flawed nature. When David's conscience was stricken by Nathan's rebuke for the evil he had done (see 2 Sam. 12), the king prayed, 'Blot out my transgressions, wash away all my iniquity and cleanse me from my sin' (Ps. 51:1-2). In just one sentence David uses three words (transgression, iniquity, sin) which bring out the basic aspects of mankind's rebellion against God. They are found in an earlier psalm where David reflects upon the blessedness of knowing God's all-encompassing forgiveness: 'Blessed is he whose transgressions are forgiven, whose sins are covered. Blessed is the man whose iniquity the Lord does not count against him.' (32:1-2).

An amazing yet logical correspondence exists between the forgiveness of which David speaks in Psalm 32 and the ministry of the Servant-Messiah in Isaiah 53. 'Transgression' comes from a verb which means 'to rebel.' The word suggests consciously defying a known law. Isaiah says the Servant was 'pierced for our transgressions' (53:5). In other words, the Messiah gave His life for those who wilfully disobeyed God. His death would be deemed sufficient to blot out the rebellious acts which we have defiantly committed against a holy God (See Num. 15:30). No estrangement is too great for His work to heal; He has redeemed us from the Law's curse (Gal. 3:13).

'Sin,' when it appears in its verbal form, means 'to miss the way.' It tells us that we have veered off course, that we have inaccurately sought the way of God. In his penitential psalm, as sin burdened David's heart, he confessed its offensiveness to God and sought His divine cleansing (51:2-4). In the Talmud it is written,

'The death of the righteous makes atonement.' David relies upon the language of atonement when he speaks of the happy one 'whose sins are covered' (Ps. 32:1). Covering and cleansing are the words of sacrifice drawing us to the altar where these benefits may be found. Ultimately they draw us to Him who 'bore the sin of many' (Isa. 53:12).

The Old Testament abounds with the ritual of sacrifice (Passover, the Day of Atonement, the Levitical injunctions) but, while preparatory to the work of the Servant, nowhere was it asserted that God, Himself, would pay the price necessary to procure man's salvation.

The Messiah's punishment brought us *shalom* (53:5) in that He bore the penalty due us for our failure to hit the mark of righteousness – to follow in God's righteous ways. His 'peace' stands for more than tranquility; it signifies wholeness, the total mending of our brokenness and the restoration of fellowship with God: 'By the blows that cut into Him, we are healed' (53:5).

Two weighty elements are connected with 'iniquity': its meaning, which suggests something twisted, and its consequence, or an element of reckoning. Iniquity forms part of our genetic makeup (Ps. 51:5); from our earliest days the intent of our heart is basically evil (Gen. 8:21). Furthermore, this iniquity requires an accounting; it must be laid to someone's account. When Stephen was being unjustly executed he prayed that God would not lay that iniquitous act to the account of his murderers (Acts 7:60). His prayer related to the matter of imputation.

David rejoices because his iniquity has not been imputed to him (Ps. 32:2); Isaiah is glad because 'the LORD has caused to land on Him [the Servant] the iniquity of us all' (Isa. 53:6). This is consonant with David's hope, for it is implicit that, if David is not to bear the consequences of his misdeeds, someone else must. Note that David does not equate blessedness with the performance of righteous acts; his hope is squarely rooted in grace (iniquity has not been laid to his account).

The Bible regards the work of the Servant-Messiah as a work of imputation. It is distinctive of the Messiah's work, however, that as sinners' deeds are laid upon Him, they, in return, receive His absolute righteousness. This latter blessedness was first known by our spiritual father, Abraham, who trusted in the Lord and was thereby considered righteous (Gen. 15:6).

Nothing taught Israel more about God's cleansing power than the Day of Atonement (*Yom Kippur*). Nothing in all of Israel's religious activities approached its significance; no ritual was as fraught with meaning. Once a year on that holiest day the High Priest would part the thick veil that separated the Temple's innermost sanctuary (The Holiest Place) from its adjacent room (The Holy Place) carrying the blood of a spotless animal. He would then sprinkle that precious blood on the Mercy Seat and seven times at the base of the Ark of the Covenant. The Mercy Seat was a rectangular slab of solid gold to which were attached two *cherubim* (symbolic winged creatures). The seat was the lid on top of the ark (a wooden box sheathed in gold), whose contents (the Law, manna, and Aaron's rod) witnessed to God's faithful provisions and relationship with Israel. The word, *mercy*, spoke to the issue of atonement; the *seat* was the place of God's enthronement (see Pss. 80:1; 99:1).

When the High Priest entered the Holiest Place it was not primarily for his own benefit; he went as a representative of each and every Israelite. His responsibility was to beseech God to forgive them – to pardon all their offences. In preparation for this event, the High Priest was moved to immaculate, isolated quarters a week before the great day. There he would be safeguarded from all forms of pollution that might render him unclean and unfit for priestly service. Only a clean priest could appear before the Holy One of Israel as the people's intercessor. To that end there were many ritual baths. The High Priest was required to bathe publicly in the presence of Israel (which he did behind a screen). According to the Talmud, he would take five complete baths during the hallowed day and wash his hands and feet ten times.

The pressing question for all who hoped in his

intercessory work was: 'Will God accept my priest's sacrifice on my behalf?' A rope was tied to the priest's leg as he entered the Holiest Place in case he had to be unceremoniously removed as a victim of God's wrath.

About two centuries following Isaiah, the prophet-priest Zechariah received a vision of a High Priest named Joshua attempting to make intercession for the nation. But to Zechariah's horror Joshua stands in the presence of God 'clothed with filthy garments' – literally, 'covered with excrement' (Zech. 3:3). And Satan (lit., 'the accuser' [3:1-2]) is there too, pointing his denouncing finger against the silent, befouled priest. Disaster seems imminent. But then the Almighty Judge rises for the defence and says, 'Take away the filthy clothes' (3:4). The priest is immediately cleansed as God freely gives him what he cannot achieve for himself. It is in that context that we are told that Joshua and his fellow priests are symbolic of a coming time when God will bring forth His Servant, the Branch (Zech. 3:8), the same unpretentious shoot from Isaiah's 'stump of Jesse' (Isa. 11:1). What is singularly striking about Zechariah's prophecy is God's promise, 'I will remove the sin of this land in a single day' (Zech. 3:9). We are reminded once again that Zechariah's word for sin (*avon*) – sin that needs to be laid to someone's account – describes what Jesus bore in His body on the cross

– 'the iniquity of us all' (Isaiah 53:6). In that day – the day of the Servant's self-sacrifice – all the morning and evening sacrifices along with the Day of Atonement will come to their intended fulfilment.

There are no remaining sacrifices, save that of praise – ' the fruit of lips that confess His name' (Heb. 13:15) – and service to the needy (Heb. 13:16).

Consider our Lord Jesus Christ. He had no washings, no isolated quarters to protect him from the world's filth. He was unbathed, spat upon and beaten. Yet He stood before His heavenly Father clean – on our behalf. Now for each soul who believes in Him the Father can say, 'Bring forth the best robe and put it on him.' Like Joshua in Zechariah's vision, the old defiled garments have been forever taken away, our sin placed upon the sin-bearing Servant. We are once more transported into the reality of Romans 8:33: 'Who will bring any charge against us? It is God who justifies.' Now we may 'draw near to God with a sincere heart in full assurance of faith, having our hearts sprinkled to cleanse us from a guilty conscience' (Heb. 10:22). Moreover God's grace has accomplished still more for us. We have become 'a holy priesthood' (1 Pet. 2:5) whose prayers God always welcomes.

We should carefully point out that what was transferred to the Messiah was not our moral deficiencies but the legal consequences of our sins; and what was transferred to us was not His perfect character and holiness but our Savior's righteous standing before His Father. This reckoning of absolute righteousness to our account is a judicial act; it is not to be identified with spiritual experiences (as meaningful as such manifestations may be). As John Walvoord wrote, 'In itself it is not an experience but a fact of divine reckoning.' [13]

Again, this is all the result of grace. All becomes ours through trusting in God's promise. At the moment of faith we can rest secure in the fact that He has borne the judgment of the law we have broken and will not impute our sins to us (2 Cor. 5:19); He has, instead, transferred His righteous standing to us (2 Cor. 5:21). Although He has, in the divine transaction, imparted to us His Holy Spirit (who effects a change in our character and conduct), our blessedness is the result of the Messiah's bearing our iniquity, not in our piling up good works. God our Father never looks at us without seeing His Son in whom He is well pleased. Our standing is as secure as the Son's – in His Father's love.

### All we like sheep...
Messiah's blessings do not come to us irrespective of our attitude. You and I are part of the criminal element for whom He died: 'Each of us has turned to his own way' (Isa. 53:6). We must turn away

from our disobedient path and turn towards God. David's experience of forgiveness followed his soul-searching acknowledgment of his sin. Until that time he knew only the misery of a heart weighed down by guilt (Ps. 32:3-5). Isaiah's message was to a people who had 'turned their backs' on God (1:4). They needed to repent, to turn from their rebellious path in the opposite direction – towards God. This about-face experience well summarizes the Hebrew idea of repentance (*shuv*) in Isaiah 55:7: '...Let him [the unrighteous] *turn* to the Lord...'.

Jesus' message of salvation was designed to make us conscious of our utter lack of a Godly righteousness (Matt. 5:3; 6:33). We enter this world bent in the wrong direction because evil is ingrained deeply within us; we were, as David said, 'brought forth in iniquity' (Ps. 51:5). None of us can change himself; God must graciously enable us to turn our backs on evil and come to Him. Jeremiah prayed, 'Restore me, and I will return' (Jer. 31:18). Even the yearning for restoration is a gift from God. The Puritan, Zachary Crofton, was right when he said that repentance is not something we can do whenever we so please; it is an evangelical grace, what Crofton called the 'operation of an Omnipotent Spirit'.

As a young man I often despaired of ever knowing God. The rituals of the synagogue were awesomely stirring, yet I continued to live 'in the land of the shadow of death' (Isa. 9:2). I spoke to my university professors about my sense of darkness but their knowledge, though philosophically erudite, could not open the way to a personal relationship with God. Then somehow the Spirit of the Lord moved me to pray, 'God of Abraham, Isaac, and Jacob, if You can be known, please reveal Yourself to me.' Soon afterwards I began reading the Scriptures and saw in the person of the Servant-Messiah the answer to my heart's most profound need. When, in the privacy of my New York apartment I was given the grace to repent of my sin and ask Jesus to be my Savior, it was not without the keen sense that my recently discovered faith was the result of God's having chosen me to know Him even before He created the world. (See Ephesians 1:4.)

As Isaiah witnessed the shameful behavior and spiritual indifference of his people the Spirit breathed a hopeful phrase through him: 'Yet, O LORD, You are our Father. We are the clay, You are the potter; we are all the work of Your hand' (64:8). God is still molding a people in accordance with His gracious will, revealing Himself to those who did not ask for Him, being found by those who did not seek Him (65:1). We worship a God who is aggressive in letting Himself be found.

# 10

## He was led like a lamb
## to the slaughter
### *Isaiah 53:7-9*

If I had lived during the days of my people's
deliverance from Pharaoh, the ritual of the
Passover lamb would doubtless have been deeply
meaningful. From the tenth until the fourteenth
day of the month of *Abib* (March/April), the
selected lamb (a young male without blemish)
would be kept at my home. It was, to be sure, a
time to observe, safeguard and protect its
flawlessness. But at another level, it was a time
to grow closer to the set apart victim. When the
moment came to kill it some form of attachment
would almost certainly have occurred (especially
for the children). The sacrificial lamb would've
been approached more like a household pet; it is
hard to imagine slaying it in the spirit of
indifference. That some form of personal identity
between victim and slayer was intended may be
assumed by later sacrificial ordinances requiring
the worshipper to 'press his hand upon the head
of the burnt offering' whose life he was offering
up to God (Lev. 1:4). In this most essential of

worshipful acts we find that which 'makes propitiation' (atonement) for sin. The animal's death 'covered over' or 'shielded' the guilty party from God's holy wrath.

As we plumb the meaning of the Messiah's death, it is incumbent upon us to identify with Him as the acceptable offering for our deliverance, 'for Christ, our Passover lamb, has been sacrificed' (1 Cor. 5:7). God's judgment passes over us as we lean on Him, our willing substitute. Like the Jews on the eve of the first Passover, we are not trusting in our good deeds or prayers or anything else – only the blood of the Lamb will spare us. Not even our degree of faithfulness forms a part of our salvation; grace has been poured out and we dwell beneath its all-sufficient covering.

There is a part of the ancient Passover liturgy which I've always found to be fascinating. Three matzohs (unleavened bread) are wrapped in a large napkin. The leader of the service reaches in and breaks the second (center) matzoh and, while all look away, he buries (hides) the broken piece. When the third cup of wine is drunk (known as the 'cup of blessing') the hidden piece is revealed to the assembled company who are permitted to partake of it. Traditional Jewish interpretation of that enigmatic event does not provide very much detail concerning its significance. Inasmuch as many first century Jews believed in Jesus, it's highly possible that the meaning of that ritual was rich in messianic symbolism. The bread itself is without leaven, a commonly used symbol for sin. Since it is the middle loaf that is broken, we may well consider the matzoh to stand for our sinless Substitute, the second member of our triune God, who was broken for us. His burial (like that of the unleavened bread) was for a short duration; He rose from among the buried on the third day. It was the traditional third cup to which Paul referred when He said, 'Is not the cup of blessing for which we give thanks a sharing in the blood of the Messiah' (1 Cor. 10:16)? In the Jewish ritual, the participation in the 'resurrected' piece of bread (called the *aphikomen*)[14] marks the end of the meal, after which nothing is to be eaten. Those who have partaken of Christ have not received a poor substitute for satisfying bread, but have delighted 'in the richest of fare' (Isa. 55:2); those who love Him know His flesh and blood to be real food and drink (John 6:55).

### An incredible response

We often hear it sung at Christmas, 'How silently, how silently, the wondrous gift is given.' The words not only fit the wondrous Incarnation but also the Servant's response to the tyrannical treatment He received. As a Jew I have followed my people's history with more than just surface curiosity. I have often marveled at Israel's cleverness and boldness in the face of adversity.

The nation has been brave and resourceful in the face of intense opposition. She has often been dismayed at the apparent silence of her Redeemer in the midst of severe trials. Two thousand years ago the Talmud recorded the reaction of the school of Rabbi Ishmael in contemplation of God's inaction to Rome's destruction of Jerusalem: 'Who is like You among the mute?' (Babylonian Talmud, *Gittin*, 56b).

But Israel has never silently endured mistreatment. And why should we expect her to? No one is predisposed to remain quiet when he is abused. Even the guilty, let alone those who are wrongly vilified, seem to want to protest their innocence. Contrary to human nature, there was no murmur of resentment against those who despised Him as He endured their oppressive judgment (53:8), a miscarriage of justice unparalleled in history. If it is rightly stated that no man ever spoke like Him, it may also be said that no stillness was ever like His. Jesus' silence before Pilate helped seal His condemnation. But, as Charles Spurgeon was quick to note, silence is the only proper response for Him who stood in the place of sinners and was, Himself, made sin (2 Cor. 5:21). There is no acceptable defence for sin when we stand before the bar of God's justice, save that of our appeal to, and reliance upon, Him who was stricken in the place of the transgressor.

Many people (my own included) have suffered

wrongly but none was sinless. The Messiah had done nothing wrong and never did a hint of anything deceitful come from His mouth (53:9). One might have expected Him to protest His innocence or to follow David's example where he cries out, 'Strike my enemies on the jaw,' or 'Let burning coals fall upon them; may they be thrown into the fire, into miry pits, never to rise' (Pss. 3:7; 140:10). The Servant sought no vengeance nor did He curse His enemies. He knew His work was with God (Isa. 49:4) and looked solely to Him for consolation.

Peter was deeply moved by his Lord's non-retaliatory example and instructs believers to endure suffering in the same commendable spirit (1 Pet. 2:20-25). A careful review of the apostle's exhortation reveals that he is calling God's people to live righteously as a result of their spiritual healing (verse 24). They are no longer like silly wayward sheep. Having been returned to the Shepherd of their souls they are expected to entrust themselves to Him when they are persecuted because of their active identification with His cause. John Selwyn, once Bishop of South Africa, was a formidable boxer in his college days. On a certain occasion he had to utter a stern rebuke to a professed convert, just recently removed from savagery. The enraged man struck the Bishop in his face with a clenched fist. Selwyn, a large, powerful man, could easily have knocked his adversary down but instead calmly awaited another blow. His confused and ashamed assailant fled into the jungle. Years later, after the Bishop had retired, the man who had struck him visited his successor to confess Christ in baptism. The new Bishop asked the man what new name he would like to take as a believer. 'Call me John Selwyn,' he replied, 'for it was he who taught me what Jesus Christ is like.'

The shepherd is a majestic figure in Israel's thinking; it is an alternate way of referring to the Messiah's kingship. Our unwillingness to return insult for insult testifies that we are a people belonging to the King. By joyfully following our Shepherd's lead in this most difficult area of discipleship we convincingly show the world that we are His chosen ones 'and precious to Him' (1 Pet. 2:4).

As a young believer I recall the testimony of Richard Wurmbrand, a pastor who was imprisoned and often beaten by his Communist captors. Once, after he was mercilessly treated and returned to his cell, the atmosphere was filled with the murmurings of other inmates as they vented their rage against the inhuman treatment he had received. But as their biting comments tapered off, the pleading voice of the pastor could still be heard – in intercession for those at whose hands he had been brutalized.

The victim of a judicial murder, 'He was cut

off from the land of the living' (53:8) as a young man. Presumably, He had left no seed. How could one possibly 'speak of His descendants'? To die without progeny was itself considered a sign of God's disfavor – even a curse. What a horrible, pitiful end for the rabbi from Nazareth – or so it seemed. He died between malefactors and so 'was assigned a grave with the wicked' (53:9). However, it is at this point that Isaiah adds an incidental, yet remarkably precise element to his prophecy: the Servant's 'assigned' place will not be the site of His interment; instead He will be 'with a rich man in His death' (53:9). The intervention of Joseph of Arimathea (Matt. 27:57-60) served as God's initial testimony to the innocence of the crucified one. Joseph is described as a godly man who was 'waiting for the kingdom of God' (Luke 23:50-51). The mighty presence of that kingdom was soon to break forth in a way that would radically transform the lives of disciples such as Joseph. But even now, in this small and undramatic episode, we see how concerned God is with details. We may take encouragement from the fact that His direct oversight of the situation is all-inclusive. How often we fret because many elements of our lives seem to be discordant or senseless. God has not lost track of the details; there are no non-essentials for Him; He 'works out everything in conformity with the purpose of His will' (Eph. 1:11), although from our restricted vantage point 'His judgments are unsearchable and His paths beyond tracing out' (Rom. 11:33).

There was a magnitude to the Servant's execution which prompted Isaiah to use the plural of 'death' (what scholars call 'a plural of amplification') in describing it (53:9). How we view death largely determines how we relate to life. Our culture's view has been well summarized by this generation's media-blitz insisting that we grab life by the throat and satisfy all our desires. We zealously pursue every type of self-satisfaction with ingenius perseverence. It is a cross-cultural attitude, embracing all socio-economic (and even religious) groups. Curiously enough, its philosophy is at least as old as ancient Egypt where archaeologists uncovered papyrus containing what appears to have been a popular ditty, circa 1300 BC (translated into contemporary speech):

> 'Don't bank down those inner fires,
>   follow out your heart's desires
>   until that day they come for you.
>   Make today a holiday – take tomorrow too –
>   You can't take it with you, Jack,
>   And when you're gone you can't come back
>   You're only going through.'

Those who believe in the Lord Jesus are imbued with the prospect of a fuller, richer life than can ever be satisfactorily described by mortal tongue.

That orientation inspired C. S. Lewis' counsel, 'We ought to give thanks for all fortune: if it is "good," because it is good, if "bad," because it works in us patience, humility and the contempt of this world and the hope of our eternal country.'[15] Lewis died of cancer (on the same day J.F. Kennedy was killed). The nurse attending him during his final days said he was uncomplaining and undemanding. It would appear that what he believed about the future had a significant effect on how he lived his final days on this earth.

Ancient rabbinic wisdom taught that when a man plastered his house he should leave a small space unfinished as a symbolic reminder that we live in an unredeemed world (Babylonian Talmud, *Bavra Bathra*, 60b). We should pray that it might be said of us that the way we lived and loved convincingly testified to our confidence in what ultimately awaits us. In the day when His glory is revealed, even 'the sun will be ashamed' (Isa. 24:23). Now we stand, along with creation, on tiptoe, anticipating the epochal event: 'new heavens and a new earth' when 'the former things will not be remembered nor will they come to mind' (Isa. 65:17).

# 11

## He will see his offspring
*Isaiah 53:9-12*

The Servant saw beyond the sorrows and suffering of His days on earth.

His vision not only concerned Himself but also envisioned a glorious future for the many who would trust in Him as their Savior. He prayed, 'Father, I want those you have given Me to be with Me where I am, and to see My glory...' (John 17:24). Far from being without offspring, He would behold a vast multitude in Heaven. A promise is only as good as the person who makes it. Isaiah assures us that there is no deceitfulness (no wicked ulterior motive) at all in God's Servant (53:9); His words are trustworthy because He is truthful.

Once when Jesus' disciples were discouraged He told them not to let their hearts be troubled (a command) for He was going to prepare a place for them. Had there been any doubt about their future, Jesus assures them that He would not have allowed them to cling to false hope (John 14:1-2). It is in that context that the Lord speaks of Himself as the way to Heaven (14:6), making it clear that He is the route of their final exodus to God. In Him is fulfilled the promise that God 'will swallow up death forever' and, with tender intimacy, individually 'wipe away the tears from all faces' (Isa. 25:8-9). Through Him the prospect of new heavens and a new earth is not a piece of pious fiction but a thoroughly believable hope.

## God's satisfaction

Although verses 10-11 may be translated in several ways, the prophet tells us that the Servant will 'be satisfied' and links that satisfaction to the certainty that 'He shall see His seed.' H. L. Ellison's translation of the text has much to commend it:

> 'He shall see His seed, He shall prolong His days,
> the will of Jehovah shall prosper in His hand.
> After the travail of His soul He shall see light and be
> satisfied...' [16]

On a parallel plane, one of the great themes of Hebrews is the work of the Messiah in bringing many sons (and daughters) to glory (Heb. 2:10). The Servant of the Lord (our salvation's Author) perfectly accomplished His task through suffering. It was 'for the joy set before Him' that He 'endured the cross, scorning its shame' (Heb. 12:2). We do well to remember that nothing was more central to the joy He anticipated than eternal fellowship with you and me. Contemplation of that truth helps us better appreciate the intensity of His passionate concern for each of us. He was motivated to offer Himself for sinners because He loved them enough to want to spend eternity with them; He considered this joy worth dying for. We may rest assured that He who laid down His life for us when we were yet rebels (Rom. 5:8) can be counted upon never to leave us or forsake us (Heb. 13:5).

### 'An offering for guilt'

How we view the Messiah's death determines our eternal destiny. Isaiah refers to it as 'a guilt (or trespass) offering' (53:10). Such an offering required the guilty to make restitution in the amount of the damage done, and to add one-fifth to the total compensation (Lev. 5:14-19). Like virtually all Old Testament sacrifices, it was designed to bring forgiveness to those 'guilty of wrongdoing against the LORD' (Lev. 5:19).

All sin is essentially against God (Ps. 51:4). We have defrauded the Lord of the honor that is due Him. How can we ever compensate the Almighty for the innumerable ways in which we have failed Him? In truth we cannot. But God's provision for us is more than adequate for our needs. Like the guilt offering, an additional value is attached to the Messiah's perfect sacrifice. It is sufficient to atone for our sins, 'and not only for ours but also for the sins of the whole world' (1 John 2:2).

When we read of it pleasing God to crush His Servant (Isa. 53:10), we are encountering a truth which is quite beyond our powers of analysis. The whole tenor of the New Testament stands against any idea of the Father's detachment from what happened upon the cross (2 Cor. 5:19), but there are moments when we are like the kings whose mouths are shut (Isa. 52:15) when it comes to explaining the mystery of what was nothing less than the death of God in our place. As a Bible teacher long ago exclaimed to his students: 'God forsaking God! Who can understand it?'

Paul prays that the Spirit of God would enable us 'to grasp how wide and long and high and deep is the love of Christ' (Eph. 3:18) so that we might be filled with His fullness (Eph. 3:19). We know that although Jesus saw the utter necessity of dying on the cross (as attested to by all four Gospels) He approached the event with a profound and fearful revulsion. There can be no denial that His experiences of deadly fear and desertion, as James Denney observed, are linked to His 'taking upon Himself the burden of the world's sin, consenting to be, and actually being, numbered with the transgressors.'[17]

A lifetime is far too short to comprehend just what good has come to us by way of that once despised Roman gibbet, but I believe a moment spent in His glorious presence – when we will indeed be filled with His fullness – will more than compensate for our current lack of understanding.

In the fortieth chapter Israel is said to have received 'double for all her sins' (40:2). Does 'double' mean she has received twice what she deserved, either in terms of her punishment or (in a positive vein) God's blessing? The former is untenable because no act of discipline is sufficient to atone for sin; death is sin's penalty (Ezek. 18:20). The 'positive' interpretation is suggested by the fact of Israel's blessedness as God's 'firstborn son' (Exod. 4:22) and Isaiah's promise (in keeping with that assigned status) of a 'double portion' (61:7). As God's children we have certainly received more than a double portion from God. In Christ, all things are ours (1 Cor. 3:21) and the future holds blessings beyond our wildest dreams (1 Cor. 2:9).

Yet, as suggested by previous comments, there is still another way to understand what it means for God's people to receive 'double for all her sins' (40:2). Dr. Allan MacRae notes that 'double' (*kephel*) may also be interpreted 'equivalent.' This makes good sense, for Isaiah is preparing us for the revelation of the divine Servant's sacrifice which is the equivalent, 'counter-balancing' provision for our sin [18] and the many trespasses it spawns. There was no other way to satisfy Heaven's righteous demands. Jesus said it emphatically, 'For I tell you, this Scripture must be fulfilled in Me, "And He was reckoned with the transgressors"; for what is written about Me has its fulfilment' (Luke 22:37).

Since the crux of the New Covenant's promise involves both the forgiveness of sin and a personal knowledge of God it should not surprise us that both of these elements appear in verse 11: 'By knowledge of Him shall My Servant, the righteous One, cause many to be accounted righteous.' This is a good translation of the text because the prophet is focusing on the Servant's bearing His people's iniquities, the chief benefit of which (our justification) does not become ours 'by His knowledge' but rather 'by [our] knowledge of Him.' God later said through Jeremiah, 'I will give you shepherds according to My heart, who will feed you with knowledge and understanding' (Jer. 3:15). There is no doubt that the prophets came to impart knowledge and understanding. But only the Messiah is able to bring people to a knowledge of God as their Father. God yearns to be known as our Father (Jer. 3:19); He desires His people to say, 'You, O LORD, are our Father' (Isa. 63:16). It is a fitting conclusion to Isaiah's many verses explaining the very personal dimension of the Servant's ministry: bringing believers into an intimate relationship with God their Father. But it is not a new idea, for Isaiah's greatest Song has already looked forward to people seeing and understanding the Servant (52:15), receiving peace and healing through Him (53:5), and being returned to the God from whose presence their sin had formerly compelled them to flee (53:6; cf. 1 Pet. 2:25). As Jeremiah would say more than a century later, 'They shall all know Me [the Lord] ... for I will forgive their iniquity and remember their sin no more' (Jer. 31:34). It bears repeating that what God offers to man through that relationship is more than a verdict of acquittal at Heaven's judgment seat; His gift to us is the unequivocal declaration of our righteousness.

Although many of the Scribes and Pharisees of Jesus' day were genuinely interested in the Law and positively sought to bring its morality to bear upon the lives of the masses (not all Pharisees were like the self-righteous character of Luke 18:11-12), the salvation they held out to the people was based on a combination of faith and personal piety. Although God commands His people to obey the Law (it is the perfect expression of His holy nature), the work of the Servant makes it clear that all human expressions of righteousness – of total obedience – fall immeasurably short of the divine requirement. Jesus resolved to be 'obedient unto death, even the death of the cross' (Phil. 2:8) that He might drink to its dregs what J.I. Packer has called 'the unique dreadfulness' of God's wrath.[19] Nothing more firmly establishes the unmerited nature of our salvation than the pierced and battered body of Him who was cursed in our place upon the tree (Gal. 3:10-14).

There have been those in Judaism's long history (including even some first century Pharisees) who would agree that none can expect to earn God's forgiveness, that obedience to the Law is nothing more than our response to a salvation provided by God's merciful covenant of salvation. [20] In an ancient daily rabbinic prayer, the suppliant prays, 'Not because of our righteous acts do we lay our supplications before Thee, but because of Thine abundant mercies. What are we? What is our piety? What is our righteousness?'

However, Jesus came announcing the presence of God in and through His person and ministry. He represents a radical departure from the point of view maintained by the Scribes and Pharisees. For Jesus is the focal point of God's revelation. As the Source of man's redemption, He takes the place of everything the people of Israel had received, including even the sacred Torah.[21] God, through a supernatural work of grace, makes us spiritually alive so that we not only trust in Jesus but also are positioned 'in Christ' (1 Cor. 1:30; Eph. 1:3). This is more than an academic matter, for the same Savior is within us. He has befriended us, has become part of our lives, and is our hope of glory (Col. 1:27). It is precisely because of His indwelling presence that God is able to write His law upon our 'inward parts' (Jer. 31:33). Although we still fail to obey God in many ways, His direct influence over us, once begun, continues throughout our lives so that we may, by His renewed initiative within us, display His splendor (Isa. 61:3). We are like transplanted trees, once barren and dying, taken from lifeless earth and given established rootage in the choicest soil.

Isaiah knows that a soul will not move in the right direction until he has been awakened by God's restorative power. Therefore the cry to repent (55:7) is based upon blessings which come to the sinner 'without money and without cost' (55:1). Nonetheless, the prophet repeatedly pleads with his people: 'Come to the God of grace that you might live!' He is bold in his appeal because God had said to him, 'My word ... will not return to Me empty, but shall accomplish what I desire and achieve the purpose for which I send it' (55:11). Whether that purpose involved the salvation of many or few (see 6:10) cannot be our primary concern. Isaiah preached with the conviction that the results were not his to achieve; God would do what pleased Him and that was satisfaction enough. Some soil may produce 'thorns and thistles' (Heb. 6:8) but an overflowing abundance will still be achieved. In the final analysis we should take comfort in the truth that the gospel is no more preached in vain than the rain which falls from Heaven (Isa. 55:10).

The Song closes with the same theme with which it began, the victory of the Servant: 'He shall see light after the travail of His soul' (53:11) and He will be given 'a portion with the great' (verse 12). Paul's message to the synagogue at Pisidian Antioch emphasized the fact that 'the holy and sure blessings promised to David' (Acts 13:34; Isa. 55:3) were confirmed in Christ when God raised Him from the dead. The eternal covenant which has been our soul's surest hope rests upon the foundational agreement subsisting between the Father and His Son. 'God raised Him from the dead, never to see decay' (Acts 13:34) in fulfilment of the good news that 'through Him everyone who believes is justified from everything (they) could not be justified from by the law of Moses' (Acts 13:39).

Where Nebuchadnezzar and Cyrus failed to achieve lasting victory, the Servant has been thoroughly successful. His kingdom will never wane but is firmly established forever. Our Conqueror has purposed to 'divide the spoils with the strong' (Isa. 53:12); He is not like the older brother (in Luke 15) who has no intention of sharing his possessions (and would feel no remorse were we to stay in our self-made pig-pens). Although all things rightly belong to Christ He does not behold His inheritance and say, 'I'll not share these blessings with such undeserving people.' To the contrary, He bids us come and receive freely that we might 'go out in joy and be led forth in peace...' (Isa. 55:12). The value of what He intends to share with us is incalculable. Isaiah said, 'Come, all you who are thirsty, come to the waters!' (55:1). In a land where water has always been an invaluable commodity, Jesus said, 'If anyone is thirsty, let him come to Me and drink. Whoever believes in Me, as the Scripture has said, streams of living water will flow from within Him' (John 7:37-38). God had promised, 'I will pour out My Spirit on your offspring, and My blessing on your descendants' (Isa. 44:3); Jesus invites us to look to Him for the gift of the Spirit which, like our justification, comes to us solely by faith (Gal. 3:14).

Although the Holy Spirit was active in the world prior to the Servant's ministry, it was on the fiftieth day after the Sabbath of Passover week, at the Jewish feast of Pentecost, that the Spirit entered into a more intimate relationship with believers (Acts 2:1-4). Peter's message to the worshiping multitudes at Jerusalem reveals once again the pivotal role of the Messiah's exaltation as a prerequisite for that outpouring: 'God has raised this Jesus to life, and we are all witnesses of the fact. Exalted to the right hand of God, He has received from the Father the promised Holy Spirit and has poured out what you now see and hear' (Acts 2:32-33).

Those who received that promise were among 'the strong' of whom Isaiah prophesied (53:12). Yet none of those who received the Spirit's animating power would have considered themselves intrinsically mighty. They would have reckoned themselves among the many 'whose weakness was turned to strength' (Heb. 11:34) by the grace of God. Rather than deny their weakness, they saw it as the means to a spiritually anointed ministry. Paul himself exemplifies the principle. God said to him, 'My grace is sufficient for you, for My power is made perfect in weakness' (2 Cor. 12:9). Like the apostle, we are no more than fragile 'jars of clay' (2 Cor. 4:7). But, as illustrated so clearly in Isaiah's early statements of comfort (chapter forty), it is our very weakness that guarantees the success of God's plan. Although we are no more resilient than cut flowers, He has committed Himself to work on behalf of those who cannot help themselves. Have we ever 'boasted' of our weakness in order that God's power might rest upon us?

A man's greatest enemy often turns out to be his strengths rather than his weaknesses. We invariably rely upon those qualities and skills we imagine ourselves to possess. The rich find it hard to enter the kingdom of God because of our culturally reinforced notion that money is power; and the clever think there's no challenge too overwhelming for them to tackle. Vast multitudes embrace 'the sword and crescent' as their banner of religious power. Untold numbers participate in obscure rituals whose symbols have long been emptied of meaning. For generations before the coming of Christ, Jerusalem's Temple had become little more than an empty shrine, its precious contents lost for ever. People worshipped at a sanctuary where not even the symbols of God's transcendent glory (Ark, Law tablets, Aaron's rod, and manna) were present to console the oft-beleaguered nation.

During the war years, Lutheran pastor Helmut Thielicke preached a series of messages to his congregation in Stuttgart. They were often interrupted by the horrors of sirens and Allied air raids. His sermons called listeners to remember their true identity by carefully studying the Person of their Savior.

Thielicke exhorted his flock 'not to become a courtesan who looks with longing glances at the glory of the mighty'. George Bernard Shaw thought that Jesus would have been far more successful had He assumed the role of a modern practical statesmen. Yet Jesus 'rose up from the place where the kingdoms of this world shimmered before Him, where crowns flashed and banners rustled, and hosts of enthusiastic people were ready to acclaim Him, and quietly walked the way of poverty and suffering of the cross.'[22] The church has often tried to accomplish her goals by following the path of human wisdom. Like Israel who early complained to Samuel that they wanted a king like all the other nations, the people of God regrettably often imitate society. They engage in power struggles (even within their own fellowship) and wind up virtually indistinguishable from the culture they are called upon to influence.

In view of God's mercy (not, as if it were possible, because we hope to earn His favor) we are to think of ourselves as 'living sacrifices' (Rom. 12:1). It is a reasonable approach to life, not patterning our aspirations and behavior after the world's but co-operating with the transforming power of God's Spirit who indwells us. Jesus poured out His life for the many whom the Father had given Him; when our thinking is right the love of God also constrains us to offer up ourselves for His children (our brothers and sisters).

It is by no means incidental that the same noun (*charis*) does double duty for the New Testament words, 'grace' and 'gratitude.' They must forever be joined together for they are as closely linked as seed and flower.

Because the Servant of the Lord gave Himself totally to His Father's will, He has been exalted far above every name and station (Phil. 2:9). I believe it is God's intention to lead each believer in a way similar to that of His Son's, in order to develop within us the passionate heart of a servant. Although we cannot die redemptively, we can live dedicatedly. Paul says, 'We always carry around in our body the death of Jesus, so that the life of Jesus may also be revealed in our body' (2 Cor. 4:10). Death precedes life; there's no way around it. God's people must live under the sign of the cross. If our heart's desire is for spiritual vitality – for joy – we must consciously identify with Him who is the fountainhead of our lives. Wisdom reduces it to a simple formula: 'He who refreshes others will himself be refreshed' (Prov. 11:25).

The particulars of servanthood will be different in each of us. We must be reluctant to prescribe exact obligations for the proper display of servanthood, lest we consign people to the monitoring of law rather than the motivation of grace. Yet, conscious of the greatness of God's grace towards us, we are motivated by the fact that the Servant continually concerns Himself with the needs (both small and great) of others:

> '... with the grief of a mother who has lost her son (Luke 7:11ff.), the predicament of a paralytic (Mark 2:1ff.), the weariness of His disciples (to whom He says, 'Come, rest a while! – Mark 6:31), and He does not fail to notice that the people who followed Him into the wilderness are hungry. He is even concerned about the wine at a wedding (John 2:1ff.). And He bestows His special love upon the seemingly worthless existences of those who are even more little than the so-called 'little people': the lepers, the lame, and the mentally ill.'[23]

Man owns and is owned by an incurably sick heart (Jer. 17); it sickens the possessor with anxiety and despair. That is why grace is the most precious word in our vocabulary. Few of us really understand grace.

If we did we wouldn't be so despondent. You see, we are far worse than we ever realize; our deceitful nature will not allow us to see the depths of our depravity (Jer. 17:9b). But – and here's the reason for joy – God's grace is far greater than we imagine. God wants us to live in the happy awareness of the fathomless depths of His grace – 'to grasp how wide and long and high and deep is the love of Christ...' (Eph. 3:18).

In the breakdown of Rome, Christianity was born. In the collapse of society, genuine life must assert its genius. As our society's once trusted forms and institutions continue to decline, those who have entrusted their lives and destiny to the Messiah have the opportunity to reveal their Master's life to an increasingly disillusioned world. There is no peace for those whose lives have been severed from God. Goethe, the so-called 'Olympian,' said in his old age that he didn't think that he had been really happy for more than a month in his entire life. Perhaps the great philosopher's vision was never elevated through beholding the dedicated lives of God's servants. There is precious little in this world to inspire or ennoble because, as Jonathan Edwards said, 'All that natural men do is wrong.' It is not, as Immanuel Kant maintained, that people know what is right (the 'categorical imperative') but simply fail to measure up to the standards; there is, as we've previously noted, a twistedness at the core of each individual which distorts and deceives even his most rudimentary thinking.

Nietzsche once said that Christians would have to look more redeemed before he would believe in their Redeemer. Now the world has no right to expect perfection from us; we are, at best, unprofitable servants. Yet, as Francis Schaeffer used to say, 'The world has a right to expect something.'

We have been given the responsibility to join Isaiah in lifting up our voices and saying, 'Behold your God' (40:9)! Something more than oral proclamations are called for; how we live must proclaim the fact that we belong to Him. Vestiges of ethics will not suffice; we must daily seek the power of the Holy Spirit whom God says He will freely give to those who ask (Luke 11:13).

# 12

## Freedom for the captives
### *Isaiah 61:1-2*

Although, strictly speaking, these words do not constitute a Servant Song, their relevance to our study of Isaiah's 'Servant' is immediately evident, framing the essence of one of Jesus' earliest public messages. Luke tells us it was delivered to those gathered on the Sabbath day in the synagogue at Nazareth. There Jesus 'stood up to read' (Luke 4:16) and was handed the scroll of Isaiah.

The synagogue (from the Greek, *synagoge*, 'a gathering together') seems to have come into being not long after the Babylonian destruction of the Temple. Jewish people needed to be anchored in their faith and revived, spiritually. Such were the needs that this ancient institution endeavored to meet. There were many of them scattered throughout the land; Jerusalem, itself, probably had several hundred. They were places for education and worship; most essentially they provided a gathering place for religious nourishment through the reading of the Law and Prophets. Although synagogues did not have appointed rabbis or ministers who would expound upon biblical texts (there were no ordained 'preachers'), each synagogue apparently had a ruler who was responsible for order and for the selection of a Scripture reader. Local residents or visitors deemed to be qualified would be called upon (or might volunteer) to read from the Scriptures and comment upon them. Jesus regularly taught in various synagogues as well as at the Temple (John 18:20) until He fell out of favor with the authorities.

According to the Talmud's *Mishnah*, the prophets were read somewhat more randomly than the Law (which was read according to a three-year cycle). Yet it was far from coincidental that Jesus received the portion of Scripture that was handed Him, for His selection from Isaiah's sixty-first chapter offered the hearer a marvelously comprehensive overview of the Servant-Messiah's mission. He concluded His reading by saying, 'Today this Scripture is fulfilled in your hearing' (Luke 4:21).

Originally addressed to Babylon's Jewish captives, Isaiah's central motif set against the 'year of Yahweh's favor' (61:2) is brim-full and overflowing with the promise of freedom. 'The year of God's favor' is the year of His acceptance – the joyful expression of His good will. It hearkens back to 'the Year of Jubilee,' the year following seven Sabbath years (viz., the 50th year), when those who were servants because of unpaid debts were set free and lands returned to their former owners (Lev. 25). It was the time for the sounding of the trumpet and the proclamation of liberty throughout the land (Lev. 25:10). So universal is the appeal of this theme that the Levitical text is inscribed upon America's Liberty Bell.

### Reason for eternal celebration

On the occasion of Messiah's birth a jubilant company of angels ascribe glory to God and praise Him for giving 'peace to men on whom His favor rests' (Luke 2:13-14). Jesus is the Anointed One, equipped to proclaim good news to the poor and heal the brokenhearted, whose proclamation of liberation frees His people from their prison house of sin. Best of all, He comes to make known the love of His Father – the fathomless depths of His favor.

We do not know the full content of Jesus' message to those gathered at the synagogue in Nazareth but we may assume, according to Isaiah's text, that He expounded upon the nature of the deliverance Isaiah promised to those bound and needy (61:1). In a later confrontation with some who had demonstrated some superficial interest in His ministry, Jesus specified His truth to be the means whereby the oppressed could be set free. In this regard He spoke of the necessity of persevering in His word to find true freedom (John 8:31). 'Then,' He said, 'you will know the truth, and the truth will set you free' (verse 32). At this point it is evident that those listening to Jesus had no appreciation for the gravity of their condition; they counter: 'We are Abraham's descendants and have never been slaves of anyone. How can you say that we shall be set free?' (verse 33). The statement runs contrary to fact. The Jews had been slaves of the Egyptians, the Philistines, the Assyrians, the Babylonians, the Persians, and, even as they spoke, of the Romans. To be sure, the Romans had given their religion formal recognition, but that did not alter the fact that Israel had nothing more than a very restricted autonomy. Nonetheless, Jesus' words were not concerned with political subjugation. He was speaking at a deeper level relating to the very core of our nature. There, too, people tend to deny the reality that they are, in the words of Wesley's hymn, 'fast bound in sin and nature's night.' John Bunyan penetratingly described sin as that burden which applies a crushing weight to those in the slough of despond.

Jesus teaches as a first principle that each of us is a sinner and is held in bondage by the power of sin (John 8:34). Counselor Paul Tournier has well remarked that advice, no matter how good it is, cannot cure us of our deepest ills:

'Advice may put people back together again, but it cannot change them. 'Advice which can touch only

131

the manner of action,' as said Ariston of old, 'can never transform the soul and set it free from its false opinions.' Advice touches the surface of personality, not the centre. It calls for an effort of the will, whereas the true cure of souls aims at the renewal of the inner affections.'[24]

Our behavior (not to mention our thoughts) proves that we are dominated by an evil power too great for us to control. Fortunately, Jesus does not leave the subject there. He immediately states that He (who brings the truth and is the truth) is uniquely able to set us free from sin's tyranny (John 8:36). Moreover He sovereignly chose to draw us to Himself. We are singularly fortunate that God has chosen us to belong to Him. Were it not so – if we chose Him – we might just as readily 'unchoose' Him in a time of moral failure. Of course, left to ourselves, we would never choose to love a holy God; like Israel we tremble when the true God draws nigh (Exod. 20:18f.).

We are always looking for life's joys in the wrong places, desiring (and exhibiting) unrestrained behavior, as if that would bring us genuine freedom. But disregard for life's restrictions cannot bring freedom from fear or guilt or evil – or from the law's just condemnation. Those alienated from God are like a churning, troubled sea (Isa. 57:20); their 'freedom' is no better than chaos.

Of all the people who ever walked the face of

this earth, none was as free as Jesus. As Lord He was free to exercise His authority as He chose to do so, yet for our sakes He willingly subjected Himself to every demand of the law. Jesus used His freedom to serve others; He found His delight in the service of others – even after His resurrection (see John 21, where the Master cooks breakfast for His weary disciples). He never demanded His rights but found His satisfaction in knowing that His Father was pleased with Him and would ultimately provide His life's necessities. We live in a time when everyone seems to be demanding their rights. The Christian who is less demanding and more content with whatever he has offers the world (as well as the believing community) a potent example of redeemed living. The late Bill Saal, former director of Arab World Ministries, said he learned two things in God's 'School of Grace': expect less from others, and love them more. These things were learned at the feet of Jesus.

## A Triune redemption

The redemption of which Isaiah prophesied was comprehensive in nature; therefore, we should not be surprised to observe its triune character: the Spirit of our heavenly Father endues His Son with power to preach and to heal (Isa. 61:1). This is one of several Isaianic passages providing a cryptic glimpse into the mystery of God's Person.

Even without the New Testament as our point of reference, Isaiah moves us in the direction of a trinitarian conception of God. In Isaiah 48:16 we hear the Messiah speaking of the fact that He was sent (again, a future event couched in the past tense) by 'the Lord God and His Spirit.' Later the Messiah is called 'the Angel (or Messenger) of God's Presence' who not only took His people's afflictions upon Himself but also patiently endured their rebellion against His Holy Spirit (Isa. 63:9-10). Thoughts such as these give a helpful backdrop for the narrative describing the launching of Jesus' public ministry:

> And when [Jesus] was praying, heaven was opened and the Holy Spirit descended on Him in bodily form like a dove. And a voice came from heaven: 'You are My Son, whom I love; with You I am well pleased' (Luke 3:21-22).

He has come to deliver a people whose afflicted minds have given way to despondency (implied in His work that will 'bind up the brokenhearted' – Isa. 61:1), and whose rebelliousness, were it not for God's compassion, precludes the possibility of emancipation.

### 'Good news to the poor'

Impoverishment comes in different forms. There is the crushing physical sort which holds untold millions in its merciless grip. There is an another

134

devastating emptiness – a spiritual impoverish-ment – which is all the more severe because its awful power may not be confined to our lifetime on earth.

When John the Baptist was imprisoned because of his stand for righteousness he sent word to Jesus asking, 'Are you the one who was to come, or should we expect someone else?' (Luke 7:20). John's view of the coming one (the Messiah) anticipated a change in the world order. He looked forward not only to a day of great news for the needy but also to 'the day of vengeance' (Isa. 61:2) when God would redress all of the wrongs in the world and repay, in kind, the evil of the Herods and the Caesars. However, if John had been present among the Nazarenes when Jesus read from Isaiah 61, he would not have heard Jesus quote the latter part of the second verse announcing the judgment of God. The time for evil's judgment had not yet come; Messiah's advent was initially an occasion for the expression of God's grace. Thus, in answering His imprisoned colleague, Jesus instructed John's messengers to tell him of the healings they had observed (see Isa. 35:5-6) and to note that the good news was being preached to the poor (Luke 7:22). Isaiah's words of impending judgment – of 'vengeance' – found partial fulfilment in the fall of Israel and the nations which oppressed her. Yet there is a day in Heaven's calendar when the full measure of God's wrath will be made manifest, when the thoughts and actions of the unrepentant and faithless will be mercilessly judged (Isa. 2:11-12; 35:4; 59:17-18; 63:4).

'He is coming, like the glory of the morning on the wave;
He is wisdom to the mighty, He is succor to the brave;
So the world shall be His footstool, and the soul of time His slave:
Our God is marching on.'[25]

There is an old expression in Hebrew, *mida keneged mida*. It literally means 'measure for measure' and refers to God's unerring judgment in repaying good and evil in kind. Paul's warning to the church falls within that context: 'Do not be deceived: God cannot be mocked. A man reaps what he sows' (Gal. 6:7).

### Blessings – for whom?

Although Jesus showed tender regard for the poor, we should bear in mind that they were not singled out simply because of their socio-economic plight. The only 'blessed poor' of which Scripture informs us are those who are 'poor in spirit' (Matt. 5:3). How one becomes 'poor in spirit' may be connected to his physical circumstances, but these are not haphazardly determined (Exod. 4:11). It cannot be denied that 'it is hard for a rich man to enter the kingdom of heaven' (Matt. 19:23); but even the rich are not beyond the reach of a sovereign loving God (verse 26). Sometimes God shows His love for a person by taking all of his life's artificial props away. Only then, it seems, is he able to seek Heaven's true riches. An anonymous poet speaks for many of us:

> 'One by one He took them from me,
> all the things I valued most,
> 'til I was empty-handed –
> every glittering toy was lost.
> And I walked earth's highways
> grieving in my rags and poverty
> until I heard His voice inviting,
> 'Lift those empty hands to Me.'
> Then I turned my hands toward heaven
> and He filled them with a store
> of His own transcendent riches
> 'til they could contain no more.
> And at last I comprehended
> with my stupid mind and dull
> that God cannot pour His riches
> into hands already full.'

It is not uncommon for the Lord to lovingly afflict us in order to drive us to Himself and a renewed commitment to do His will. Drawing from his own experience, the psalmist says, 'Before I was afflicted I went astray, but now I obey Your word.... It was good for me to be afflicted so that I might learn Your decrees' (Ps. 119:67, 71).

### In Search of Riches
Although 'God has chosen those who are poor in the eyes of the world to be rich in faith' (Jas. 2:5), this truth does not undercut the fact that there are

numberless poor people who have little interest in God and whose daily hope is centered in little more than the possibility that they may have bought a winning lottery ticket. Spiritual blindness cuts across all social, ethnic, and religious groups. God must open the heart before it can receive His good news; unless He does, our minds will not seize upon His message of hope.

It is solely His undeserved favor that constrains us to believe that the Messiah left His riches in glory and became poor so that we through His poverty might become rich (2 Cor. 8:9). This is more than a point of doctrine; it should help us gain a more insightful understanding of what God considers most valuable. How beautifully are our Maker's values revealed by the psalmist:

> 'He heals the brokenhearted
> and binds up their wounds.
> He determines the number of the stars
> and calls them each by name' (Psalm 147:3-4).

Even the massive galaxies take second place to God's primary concern.

Nothing takes precedence over the needs of the brokenhearted. There is no doubt of that for God allowed His own heart to be broken upon the cross that healing may come to us – 'by His wounds we are healed' (Isa. 53:5).

### 'To preach and to proclaim'

How do you bind up an invisible heart-wound? The Book of Proverbs says, 'Death and life are in the power of the tongue' and that 'Good words can make an anxious heart glad' (18:21; 12:25). They can even bring 'healing to the bones' (16:24). But to bring release to sightless prisoners (Isa. 61:1) the speaker must possess far more than even the most consummate verbal skills.

Those who opposed Jesus could not deny the authority bound up with His words. Once in the city of Capernaum, a paralytic was brought to Him. Jesus said to him, 'Take heart, son; your sins are forgiven' (Matt. 9:2). Some of the Scribes were critical of Jesus. How could a mere man make such an authoritative pronouncement? How could any human being accurately assess the guilt of another and its influence upon his physical predicament? Jesus, knowing their thoughts, said to them, 'Which is easier: to say, "Your sins are forgiven," or to say, "Get up and walk"?' (verse 5). The Scribes knew that the former statement could be more easily said, for it pertained to unseen realities. On the other hand, to say 'Rise and walk' would present a formidable difficulty for the speaker's credibility could not escape instant evaluation. It was then that Jesus healed the crippled man and put to flight any doubts as to the legitimacy of His proclamation. Jesus' words were proved to be invested with divine authority. His credentials were unimpeachable.

In the Hebrew Old Testament, *dabar* may be translated either 'word' or 'deed.' In the ministry of the Messiah, His word, like that of His Father's, achieved the deed it was spoken to accomplish. (See Isa. 55:10-11.)

Our encouragement as His people is derived from our Lord's authority and credibility. He was never dishonest, sly, or insincere; never did the Teacher prevaricate in the slightest (Isa. 53:9). His word is truth and is backed by all the powers of Heaven. Now that word calls all people to repent and believingly cleave to Him while we still live in 'the year of God's favor.'

### 'Make me a captive. Lord...'

There is a place in Pasternak's *Doctor Zhivago* where the hero observes that a person under Communist rule can only find freedom in a concentration camp – that imprisonment brings with it a certain kind of liberty. An authentic spiritual life takes this same principle as foundational: there is no freedom as long as we live to please ourselves; we are designed to serve God.

Malcolm Muggeridge has pointed out that the way of life 'begins where for Christ, Himself, its mortal part ended – at the cross'.

'There alone, with all our earthly defences down and our earthly pretensions relinquished, we can confront

140

the true circumstances of our being; there alone grasp the triviality of these seemingly so majestic achievements of ours, like going to the moon, unravelling our genes, fitting one another with each other's hearts, livers, and kidneys.'[26]

It is as we confront the Servant's cross that we behold our Master's earthly destiny and His link to Glory. It is as we contemplate the biblical meaning of the cross that everything else occupies its proper place. There we behold the God-Man, bleeding and dying for the seed promised Him (Isa. 53:10). 'Jesus died as setting up a magnetic pylon, drawing all hearts unto Him...'[27] It was there on the Cross that the blood of the Servant became, as it were, a cleansing stream to wash away the defilement of all who would look up to Him in faith. Sir Arthur Conan Doyle (of Sherlock Holmes' fame) dismissed the gospel as 'too bloody' for his tastes, yet untold millions – Jews and Gentiles alike – have found in that poured out life God's purifying stream. His was the punishment by which God's peace became ours (Isa. 53:5). The physician in Shakespeare's *Macbeth* is asked:

'Canst thou not minister to a mind diseased,
Pluck from the memory a rooted sorrow,
Raze out the written troubles of the brain,
And with some sweet oblivious antidote
Cleanse the stuff'd bosom of that perilous stuff
Which weighs upon the heart?'

The timeless burden of mankind, so deeply ingrained within Macbeth, desperately seeks supernatural healing. In an ancient Greek myth, the mighty Hercules was given the task of cleaning the collected filth from the famous Augean stables where generations of renowned horses had been bred. He met the immense challenge by diverting a great river through the stalls.

But no mythological elements attend the feat accomplished by the Messiah when 'blood and water' flowed from His pierced side (John 19:34) in order that He might 'redeem us from all wickedness and purify for Himself a people that are His very own...' (Tit. 2:14). Paul finishes his phrase with the observation that those for whom the Messiah gave His life are now 'eager to do what is good.' The tide that washes humankind clean brings renewal and reorientation. Jesus' sin-removing love is a love that beckons us: 'Follow Me.'

### 'Behold Me; send Me' (Isa. 6:8)

So pressing was the call to repentance and the coming of cataclysmic events that Isaiah does not relate his call to service until the sixth chapter.

While it is altogether supernatural, it is altogether real in time and space. Isaiah ministered during the reigns of Uzziah, Jotham, Ahaz, and Hezekiah. It is within the context of history, while the first of these kings was still enthroned, that the prophet records his life changing experience:

it was in the twelfth year of Jotham's co-regency with Uzziah, in the thirteenth year of Pekah of Israel (740 BC), that Isaiah saw the Messiah. (See John 12:41.)

His vision of God is terrifying. He trembles before a holy God. Inanimate objects shake as the *seraphim* (lit., 'burning ones') cover themselves in the presence of the Holy One of Israel. Did they behold in some cryptic form the Lamb slain from before the world's creation? We might well say of them along with the hymnist: 'No angel in the sky can fully bear that sight, but downward bends his burning eye at mysteries so bright.'

Isaiah fears for his life as he cries out, 'A man – unclean of lips am I!' (6:5). He is like Job, whose vision of God caused him to abhor himself (Job 42:5-6). But God does not destroy Isaiah; instead, He tells him that his sin has been atoned for (Isa. 6:7). It is because of his cleansing that Isaiah is able to offer his service to God. Before he was reconciled to God through the benefits of the altar (a word meaning 'place of the slaughter') Isaiah could not even enter into the seraphim's worship of the Almighty, let alone serve Him. The prophet's experience of God's cleansing power immediately causes him humbly to offer his service to the God of grace.

Unforgiven sin is an obstacle to service. David prayed that God would create a clean heart within him (Ps. 51:10); then he would dedicate his energies to teaching God's ways to other sinners (Ps. 51:13). Of course, until a soul is reconciled to God there is no interest in either praising Him or serving Him. Service rises out of our knowledge of God which, as we have seen, is the result of forgiveness.

The mysterious *seraphim* (their biblical appearance is unique to Isaiah 6) fly quickly to do God's will, all the time covering their faces and feet in self-effacement. They manifest two essential qualities of servanthood: promptness and humility.

When Isaiah hears the voice of the Lord saying, 'Whom shall I send? And who will go for us?,' he knows that God is calling him to a demanding and oft-times thankless task. His ministry will be similar to the Servant of the Lord's in that the people will reject His word (Isa. 6:9-10). But the means and the results are all in the hands of *Yahweh Shabayot* – 'of Hosts' (6:3), a name conveying God's absolute control over all things, seen or unseen, in heaven or on earth. Even the infinitesimal particle has no free reign in the kingdom of the Almighty. 'In [Christ] all things hold together' (Col. 1:17); He sovereignly oversees all things – and He holds you together. In his *How to Give Away Your Faith*, Paul Little strikes at the matter's core: 'The statement that God is in control is either true or it's not true. If it's not true, we'd better forget about God. But if it is true and we accept God's revelation of Himself, our faith enables us to enjoy and rest in the certainty of His providence.'

With hope, love and trust you may join Isaiah and boldly embrace whatever work God calls you to do. Respond quickly to His call (delay is the handmaid of disobedience) and rejoice in remembering that 'neither he who plants nor he who waters is anything, but only God, who makes things grow' (1 Cor. 3:7).

# 13

## Realising our true identity

*But you, Israel, are My servant,*
*Jacob whom I have chosen,*
*you descendants of Abraham My friend*
(Isa. 41:8).

Israel's failure to live up to her high and noble calling (Isa. 42:19) potently underscores the fallenness of man. Like Adam, she was given the privilege of a personal relationship with the Almighty, yet chose the disastrous path of disobedience. How strange that in spite of Israel's history Jewish theologians have refused to believe that man is a radically fallen creature.

It was a great honor to receive God's law; it was also a heavy burden. Stephen's blunt and illuminating address to the Sanhedrin acknowledges both facts by simultaneously pointing both to the law's heavenly origin and Israel's failure to keep it (Acts 7:53). God brought His people out of Egypt to be His very special possession; they belonged to Him (Deut. 7:6). Israel recognized her obligation to serve God; they declared to Moses, 'All the words which the LORD has said we will do' (Exod. 24:3). But she quickly fell into the most grievous idolatry, blind prisoners of base impulses which, apart from God's grace, would damn us all. Israel's enthusiastically spoken intentions found no corresponding reality; Isaiah said she 'yielded only bad fruit' (5:2).

Enter the Servant who does battle on behalf of those weakened and warped by sin. His delight is in the law of God but, unlike even the zealous psalmist (who also loves God's law), He does not have to say, 'I have gone astray like a lost sheep...' (Ps. 119:176). In the Messiah's complete obedience may be found our perfect righteousness. 'The righteousness of God' was an expression that once filled Martin Luther with hate and fear until he grasped the truth that, through grace and sheer mercy, God's righteousness is made ours through the simple instrument of faith. 'Not my own efforts,' said Alexander MacLaren, 'but the influx of that pardoning cleansing grace which is in Christ will wash away the accumulation of years, and the ingrained evil which has stained every part of my being.' Our warfare is ended; the battle has been won for us. Just as God brought His own out of the land of Egypt, the house of bondage, He has brought us out of the prison house (Isa. 42:7). He did not come for the self-satisfied — for those who are contented with themselves and their spiritual accomplishments. The Lord has come to serve the needs of the mournful, whose grief in life is in no small way related to their deeply ingrained sense of failure. His comfort is not for those who have it all together; it's for those who are broken and know it (Matt. 5:4). His pastoral embrace is for those whose dreams have been destroyed by life's harsh realities; their cries are not treated indifferently by our compassionate God (Ps. 34:18). Let Wesley's testimony be ours: 'He owns me for His child; I can no longer fear.... With confidence I now draw nigh, and "Father, *Abba*, Father!" cry.'[28]

The law – the revelation of our crookedness – no longer exercises its fearful tyranny over us because we have satisfied its total demands in the person of Christ Jesus. It is as if we had personally fulfilled every jot and tittle of the law's demands. Yet the One who has taken up our cause and rescued us from our dark, ignoble past calls us to serve our Redeemer with grateful hearts. This is no longer a fearful enterprise because God, Himself, has removed all possibility of failure. Our judgment has been borne by Him who has blotted out our sins and promised not to remember them (Isa. 43:25). Moreover He pours His Spirit upon us (44:3) while He tenderly carries us 'close to His heart' (40:11). Most important, He has repeatedly given His word never to forsake us (Isa. 41:17; 42:16; Heb. 13:5).

On this confident note we stand ready to respond to the call to 'live as servants of God' (1

Pet. 2:16), to join Isaiah in asking God to send us to serve Him, knowing that whatever He gives us to do will not only serve His purposes but also bring true *shalom* (wholeness) to us. An old friend of mine discovered a wonderful dimension to that truth when he was hospitalized and scheduled for surgery because of his ulcerative stomach. The night before his operation he rose from his bed to pray for other patients whose moans had drawn his attention. Somewhere along the way, as he prayed for the healing of others, his own body was restored to health. Inexplicably, the Lord had dramatically ministered to him as he focused upon the needs of others. It is not uncommon to find unexpected blessings along the path of servanthood, for 'he who refreshes others will himself be refreshed' (Prov. 11:25).

## Reprise: the refreshing essentials

We have reviewed some of the chief character-istics of *the Servant of the Lord*, being mindful of the fact that God's redemptive purpose is not only to spare us from judgment but also to reproduce the character of His Son within us. He has set us free from sin that we might become His righteous servants (Rom. 6:18, 22). And in carefully exam-ining Isaiah's Servant Songs we behold the many dimensions of that desired righteousness.

The call to take up our cross daily and follow our Lord is not easily accomplished. None of us naturally takes to self-denial. Our personal desires are often in conflict with that which we know to be right. The cry of the apostle strikes a responsive chord: ' I do not understand what I do. For what I want to do I do not do, but what I hate I do' (Rom. 7:15). But Paul does not end on that despairing note. His rescue from that relentless cycle of disobedience is found in the Messiah who rescues him from this body of death (7:24-25). It is on that basis that Paul can appeal to us to dedicate ourselves to God's service; the apostle thinks of it as a 'reasonable' response to God's mercy (12:1). Therefore we serve Him simply because we love Him; any other motivation casts us adrift from scriptural truth.

The enriching nature of the Servant Songs notwithstanding, our many references to the New Testament throughout this book is a strong reminder that, as foundational as the Old Testament revelation is, the prophets possessed only partial understanding of the Messiah's work. Bible scholar, Ray Dillard, used to say that one of the functions of the Old Testament is to disappoint us. It was one way of telling seminarians that we cannot learn all we need to know about the Lord without the New Testament, whose writings constitute our unique, primary source of testimony to the person, teaching and saving work of Jesus Christ. Old Testament expositor, Franz Delitzsch, said much the same thing when he taught that, apart from the New Testament's commentary, we would be severely limited in our understanding of Isaiah.[29] F.F. Bruce sums up the value of these thoughts in his wise warning, 'to sit loose to the New Testament is thus to sit loose to the Christ to whom it bears witness';[30] and to sit loose to Him is to live sadly deficient, unproductive lives.

Isaiah begins his first Song of the Servant with the words, 'Behold My Servant, I uphold Him continually' (42:1). There was a potent invisible sustaining link between the Servant and His Father; that same link is the supporting force in our lives as well. It would be a sad commentary on our God's saving power if, having brought us out of our own personal 'Egypts', He left us to flounder about on our own. But God wants us to rest confidently in the fact that, having begun a good work in us, He will carry it on to completion (Phil. 1:6). Were it not for His undergirding hand all our striving to serve Him would constitute an exercise in futility. And were it not for the Scriptures which reveal His power and purposes we should not have the faintest idea concerning how His grace functions and stimulates us to accomplish His will.

Isaiah's younger contemporary, Amos, spoke of a mournful time when people would thirst for God's Word but not be able to find it (Amos 8:11-12). People always run the risk of eventually forfeiting that which they repeatedly devalue – to their everlasting sorrow. As a child I made light of my piano teacher's efforts to get me to read the music as it was written (not as I liked to improvise upon it). After many lessons she finally told me she had decided not to teach me any more. Years later I regretted having lost her profound musical insights, but her decision was reasonable considering my apathetic response to her many entreaties. What one greets indifferently may one day be altogether taken from him.

## Name above all names

As I review the Servant passages and consider the many inspiring qualities of the Messiah there is one particularly significant force that binds them all together, a force bound up with His very Name. Messiah is a title derived from the Hebrew, *mashiach*, a verbal adjective meaning 'anointed one.' Israel's practice of ceremonially anointing their leaders with oil symbolically anticipated the unlimited outpouring of the Holy Spirit on that quintessential ruler who would bear the name Messiah.

There is no doubt that the Holy Spirit is God's provision to enable us to think and act consonantly with His will. It is easy to take the work of the Spirit for granted – to forget to ask for His anointing upon all that we imagine, say, and do. That is why I have stressed the importance of seeking the power of His Holy Spirit every day if our servanthood is to ring true to God's intentions.

Through the finished and applied work of the Servant we are able to respond to His grand invitation: 'Come, all you who are thirsty, come to the waters' (Isa. 55:1). It is easy to recognize thirst in a dry climate, but in our day-to-day frenetic lives we sometimes don't realize that most of us are walking about terribly dehydrated. God forbid that our spiritual thirst is ever fully assuaged, for Jesus has invited us to come and drink from Him continually (John 7:37).

## Seeing the distant land

While viewing the transformed future Isaiah takes note of a distant landscape where the ugly thornbush is replaced by the pine tree, and myrtles take the place of briers (Isa. 55:13). Again, the prophet is not simply offering us a lesson in divinely altered topography (see 40:4). God's saving work involves the uprooting of the old and planting the new (Jer. 1:10). That which is freshly planted stands in regular need of heaven's moisture. But the same holds true for life at all stages of development. We need to seek Him who is 'like streams of water in the desert' (Isa. 32:2). Gerard Manley Hopkins prayed, 'O Lord of My life, send my roots rain!' A. W. Tozer, in *Man, the Dwelling Place for God*, tells of his ongoing prayer for that 'jubilant pining and longing for

God.' Tozer believed that the evangelical churches had their doctrines straight but lamented, 'This longing for God that brings spiritual torrents and whirlwinds of seeking and self-denial – this is almost gone from our midst.'

The Holy Spirit was not poured out upon the Servant for the sake of His emotional contentment or titillation but, rather, for the sake of serving His Father effectively in the world. The Spirit came upon Him to anoint His ministry to the poor and needy whom the Father sent Him to redeem (Isa. 61:1). We must disabuse ourselves of the notion that the fullness of the Spirit may be experienced by any believer irrespective of his inward motivation. Although the full extent of His rich and freely given grace is beyond calculation, we severely confine our experience of the Spirit's plenitude unless our heart's desire is to glorify God in our service, whether that service is directed heavenward in worship or towards the many 'bruised reeds' and 'smoldering wicks' who, like us, so desperately need to know His saving love.

**'Arise, shine, for your light has come...' (Isa. 60:1)**
I've often thought the matter of serving God is well symbolized in the festival of *Chanukah* ('dedication'), which celebrates Israel's victory over Syrian adversaries in 165 BC. The celebration focuses upon the rededication of the Temple. In modern times a *menorah* holding eight candle-

sticks stands center-stage. For eight consecutive days each of the candles is lit in commemoration of the ancient deliverance. An extra candle (called *shamash*, the 'servant' light) is used to light each adjacent candle. The ceremony should remind us that we must receive our light from another – from Him who is 'the light of the world' (John 8:12). Paul tells us that we are all 'sons of the light' (1 Thess. 5:5). This is because our lives are bound up with the life of our Savior; we are 'light *in* the Lord' (Eph. 5:8). It is imperative that God's truth shine through us so that many will recognize its divine source and embrace that light (Isa. 60:3). Like the high priest, Aaron, we should ask the Lord to make His face shine upon His people (Num. 6:25). We are among those upon whom God's great light has dawned, but we need to have that light continually rekindled within us in order that, by His grace, we may reflect it to those who still dwell 'in the land of the shadow of death' (Isa. 9:2). Reinhold Niebuhr taught his students that 'love is purest when it desires no returns for itself; and it is most potent where it is purest.' If we would serve the Almighty well, we must allow His pure disinterested benevolence to shine forth from within us. In that way will the Lord reveal Himself to the world and 'His righteousness will be like a garden in early spring, filled with young plants springing up everywhere' (Isa. 61:11, New Living Translation).

Part of the Bible's vision for a distant age sees Israel moved to jealousy over the good news of the Messiah's justifying love. Moses said of his people, 'I will make you envious by those who are not a nation...' (Rom. 10:19). That which produces personal envy is essentially the same from age to age. Affluency and health come up short in answering the soul's deepest needs. Individuals desire peace (the Hebrew concept of *shalom* – wholeness) and what G. K. Chesterton called 'the giant secret of the Christian' – joy (minimally, a sense of stable wellbeing in the midst of strife). These qualities should be observable in the lives of those who have put their faith in Jesus Christ. There are many of Israel who cannot see the light of Christ in His church. Past persecutions and intolerance fill their remembrances; the present reality of the Servant is too obscure for them to discern. Unless our love is expressed in tangible ways (and is not that expression an overflow of His peace and joy within us?) we can hardly expect our verbal proclamations to be widely effectual.

The prophet realizes that God's comfort is never something to take for granted — that He who has the power to save also causes many to 'fall and be broken' (Isa. 8:15). Luke tells us that when Joseph and Mary first came to the Temple with their infant they heard devout Simeon say, 'this child is destined to cause the falling and rising of many...' (Luke 2:34). Some will speak against Him while others (like Simeon) will rejoice in His salvation. Although these issues of response must ultimately rest with Him who alone can draw souls to Himself (John 6:44), we must not ignore Isaiah's mandate: 'Lift up your voice ... do not be afraid' (Isa. 40:9). There are far too many gospel heralds who always seem to be apologizing for their message and straining to reconcile it with popular notions of spiritual reality. Bible expositor, Alexander MacLaren, observed that we all have a tendency to speak the truth less confidently where we know people will oppose it, but he warned all believers to guard against cowardice where God's glory is concerned. While we should present the truth with gentleness and meekness (2 Tim. 2:25), we must never compromise with respect to God's truth.

Unto us is committed the gospel message. All need to hear it, for their eternal destiny is bound up with it – and with Him, the very embodiment of Good News. Like Anna, whose thanks to God for the birth of her Savior was expressed in her outspokenness of Messiah's presence in the world (Luke 2:38), may the reality of the Servant's saving love constrain us to affirm with enlightened Simeon: 'He is a light to reveal God to the nations, and He is the glory of [God's] people Israel' (Luke 2:32, New Living Translation). There are many who are still 'waiting for the consolation of Israel'

157

(Luke 2:25). They need to learn of the comfort that has been provided in Christ that they might trust in His finished work. We can do no greater service than to point them (Jew and Gentile alike) to Him who delights in freeing His people from the weight of their sin, whose consolation is nothing less than the restoration of fellowship with God. Our message is one of redeeming grace: God suffered for us – in our place – and there's nothing left for us to do but gratefully receive His gift. His obedience and sacrifice have won the day; whatever service we bring is but our thankful response for what He has done.

Unfortunately, there are far too many believers who've lost track of the fact that the performance of Christ on the cross alone serves as the foundation of our standing with God. Author Jeff VanVonderen correctly notes that although 'we pay lip-service to the idea that we're accepted because of God's grace, the struggle for acceptance on the basis of works is epidemic'.[31] And sometimes it is within the so-called evangelical structures that we encounter sermons, books, and seminars stressing performance as the key to being truly accepted by God.

When the Servant Songs are studied along with their New Testament counterparts, the inescapable conclusion is that we are saved by simple confidence in Jesus' work – plus nothing.

## Notes

1. *Beth Emeth* means 'House of Truth.'

2. My quotations from Scripture, when not following the NIV, try to reflect a literal rendering of the Hebrew text.

3. Dillard and Longman, *An Introduction to the Old Testament* (Zondervan, 1994).

4. Babylonian Talmud, *Sanhedrin*, 98b.

5. Quoted by Malcolm Muggeridge in *Jesus Rediscovered* (Doubleday, 1969).

6. From *Deep Is the Rock* (Elms Court: Arthur H. Stockwell Limited, 1966).

7. One of the 456 passages which ancient rabbinical authorities once considered 'Messianic.'

8. P.T. Forsyth, *The Work of Christ* (Hodder & Stoughton, 1910).

9. P.T. Forsyth, *The Person and Place of Jesus Christ* (From his lectures in London, England).

10. John R.W. Stott, *The Cross of Christ* (InterVarsity Press, 1986).

11. P.T. Forsyth, *Justification of God* (Duckworth, 1916).

12. Babylonian Talmud, tractacte *Sanhedrin* 98b.

13. John F. Walvoord, Article on 'Imputation' in *Baker's Dictionary of Theology*, 1972.

14. Usually taken to mean 'dessert,' I have heard a Jewish-Christian trace its meaning to an expression meaning, 'I came!'

15. C.S. Lewis, *Letter to Don Giovanni Calabria* (10 August, 1948).

16. H.L. Ellison, *The Servant of Jehovah*, (Letchworth Printers Ltd, N.D.).

17. James Denney, *The Death of Christ*, (Tyndale Press, 1970).

18. Allan MacRae, *The Gospel of Isaiah* (Moody Press, 1977).

19. J.I. Packer, *Knowing God*, (InterVarsity Press, 1979).

20. E.P. Sanders, *Paul and Palestinian Judaism* (Philadelphia: Fortress, 1977).

21. D.A. Hagner, *The Jewish Reclamation of Jesus* (Academie: Zondervan, 1984).

22. Helmut Thielicke, *Our Heavenly Father*, (Baker Book House, 1974).

23. Thielicke, *op. cit.*

24. Paul Tournier, *Escape from Loneliness* (Westminster Press, 1962).

25. From Julia Ward Howe's, *Battle Hymn of the Republic.*

26. Malcolm Muggeridge, *Jesus Rediscovered* (Doubleday, 1969).

27. R.E.O. White, *The Night He was Betrayed* (Eerdmans, 1982).

28. From the hymn, *Arise, my soul, arise* by Charles Wesley (1742)

29. Franz Delitzsch, *Commentary on Isaiah* (T. & T. Clark, 1902).

30. F.F. Bruce, *A Mind for What Matters* (Eerdmans, 1990).

31. Jeff VanVonderen, *Tired of Trying to Measure Up* (Bethany House Publ, 1989).